Accountability Through Student Tracking: A Review of the Literature

Compiled by

Jim Palmer
Associate Director
Center for Community College Education
George Mason University
and
AACJC Senior Fellow

American Association of Community and Junior Colleges
1990

Accountability Through Student Tracking:
A Review of the Literature

Published by the American Association of Community and Junior Colleges, 1990
National Center for Higher Education
One Dupont Circle, N.W., Suite 410
Washington, D.C. 20036
(202) 728-0200

Printed in the U.S.A.

ISBN-87117-219-4

Library of Congress Catalog Card Number: 90-83992

This project has been partially underwritten by the generous support of the U.S. Department of Education's Fund for the Improvement of Postsecondary Education (FIPSE). The opinions expressed herein, however, do not necessarily reflect the policy of the Department of Education or FIPSE.

TABLE OF CONTENTS

LIST OF FIGURES

LIST OF TABLES

FOREWORD

In 1988 the Fund for the Improvement of Postsecondary Education (FIPSE) awarded the American Association of Community and Junior Colleges (AACJC) a three-year grant for a project aimed at determining what works in implementing student tracking systems--data bases that identify the attributes of entering community college students, track student progress toward those goals on a term-by-term basis, and provide informational feedback for institutional planning and improvement. Over the course of three years, AACJC was to design a model student tracking system, implement it at community colleges where none is in place, and assess the factors that impede or contribute to the implementation process. In the abstract, the project appears straightforward, with the three project components—design, implementation, and analysis—following logically to the desired end: a better understanding of the implementation process. But the past year's experience has proven more difficult than this straightforward plan implies, and as a result the project, though informative, has in some ways evolved differently than originally intended.

A major difficulty was developing a comprehensive tracking model that goes beyond suggestions for data elements—those variables that might be included in the tracking system—and tackles the problem of implementation and use. It is one thing to say that a tracking system should include data on student educational goals, grade point averages, course completion rates, and other indicators of student progress and success. But the tasks of building a computerized data base and of using the data once they are generated pose their own problems, complicated by the incompatibility of computer hardware and software from campus to campus and by the varying political environments institutional researchers face in collecting and reporting data. As a result, this monograph does not provide a model tracking system for use nationwide, as our original proposal intended. Drawing instead upon selected writings and other sources, the following pages bring student tracking into a larger, more theoretical perspective, examining the potential role of tracking systems in student outcomes research, the limited scope of community college longitudinal studies conducted to date, and the problems encountered by those who have worked on the development of student tracking systems. While the monograph provides no panacea for institutional researchers—no quick, easy, and portable tracking system that can be readily adopted—it outlines many of the factors to be considered in longitudinally tracking student progress and points the reader to sources of further information.

As community college researchers gain experience with tracking systems, augmenting current data collection activities with longitudinal looks at student flow and outcomes, the theoretical discussions presented here will be supplemented by more practical, how-to information. The LONESTAR student tracking system recently implemented at the Texas community colleges (and discussed in Part Four of the monograph) is the largest experiment to date, undoubtedly paving the way for the implementation of longitudinal student data bases at other colleges nationwide. The published descriptions of LONESTAR (Ewell, Parker, and Jones, 1988; National Center for Higher Education Management Systems, 1988a, 1988b) are by themselves signal contributions, providing an excellent description of the technical processes involved in designing a tracking system and generating reports on student progress. On a more limited scale, AACJC's FIPSE-sponsored project should also contribute, utilizing the experiences of ten participating colleges (who are developing their own tracking systems) to determine what works in their design and implementation. Until these and other projects develop over time, little can be said with certainty about the degree to which tracking systems will become a permanent fixture in practice. As Bers (1989) concludes in her monograph on Using Student Tracking Systems Effectively:

> Tracking students through postsecondary education is clearly receiving attention
> and resources. It will probably be at least another half decade before fully integrated

systems are in place, tested and refined. Only then will educators be in a position
to assess whether the projected benefits warrant the obvious costs (p. 7).

While reading this monograph, several caveats should be kept in mind. First, the monograph draws upon available literature only. Thus, many unpublished research efforts, however excellent, go unmentioned. Second, the monograph cites—for illustrative purposes—only a selection of institutional research projects undertaken to assess student flow and progress. The omission of other projects should not be interpreted as a negative assessment of those projects. Third, no attempt has been made to provide thorough or exhaustive descriptions of the research projects that <u>are</u> cited. Readers who want further information on the full scope of those projects should turn to the source documents listed in the "References" section.

Several individuals reviewed all or parts of the manuscript and provided helpful suggestions for improvement: Dennis Jones of the National Center for Higher Education Management Systems, Washington, D.C.; Janis Cox Jones of the Los Rios Community College District, California; Lisa Kleiman of Tidewater Community College, Virginia; John Losak of Miami-Dade Community College, Florida; and Daniel McConochie of the Maryland State Board for Community Colleges. I am grateful for their assistance. Any errors or omissions, however, are my responsibility alone.

Finally, I acknowledge the assistance of the Fund for the Improvement of Postsecondary Education for underwriting the costs of producing this monograph. The opinions expressed on the following pages, however, are not necessarily endorsed by the reviewers of the manuscript, by FIPSE, or by the United States Department of Education.

Jim Palmer

PART ONE:

THE CHALLENGE OF ACCOUNTABILITY

THE CHALLENGE OF ACCOUNTABILITY

Since 1983, when the U.S. Department of Education released *A Nation at Risk*, "reform" has become the leitmotif of educational policy makers. As Coffey (1989) points out,

> Calls for higher standards and tougher performance criteria have trumpeted from both within and without the education establishment. Something is wrong with American education, the critics charge, and institutional defenders seem hard-pressed to meet the criticism with much more than rhetoric about the face validity and the utility and value of higher education and the difficulty in measuring educational outcomes (p. 2).

Once again, educators are being asked for an accounting of how education dollars are spent, for indicators of the dividends that investment yields, and for evidence of good faith efforts to improve practice.

Following the expansion of higher education in the 1960s, today's calls for reform stress student assessment and placement as a necessary condition of access. This is evident in a number of state-sponsored reform proposals (outlined by Bragg, 1989), which often stress the use of proficiency tests, both at entrance and exit. These reforms have a two-fold intent. One is to provide students with more directed educational experiences founded on clearly defined prerequisites, curricular paths, and outcomes. The second goal is accountability through the documentation of student outcomes. Underlying both goals is a sense that increased access to college, while laudable, must translate into increased access to education, with students making demonstrable progress through a rigorously structured curriculum.

This two-part reform effort has been keenly felt at open-access community colleges. Placement testing, mandatory remediation (where necessary), and enforced standards of academic progress are increasingly viewed as more appropriate alternatives to the laissez-faire, freedom-to-fail approach to student matriculation that prevailed at community colleges in the 1970s. By the same token, institutional researchers and others collecting data have been urged to shift their emphasis from enrollment, dollars expended, and other indicators of quantity to longitudinal looks at student flow and progress. Unlimited access without documented benefits has become fiscally, and hence politically, untenable. As Carter (1986) explains, "While the humanistic philosophies of open access and equal opportunity are indeed noble gestures, their cost must be justified" (p. 89). She goes on to note that "research must respond to the questions of success or failure that are generated by studies of students and programs" (p. 95).

Matriculation

A key result of today's emphasis on achievement has been the attempt to tighten student matriculation policies by requiring students to identify their goals and follow an ordered, sequential path toward their completion. These policies are in large part a reaction against enrollment trends of the 1970s, an era in which fewer students followed traditional course sequences and in which "the pattern of sequential attendance through first introductory, then advanced courses was in decisive retreat" (Cohen and Brawer, 1982, p. 62). Recognizing that many students may need more guidance and that ad hoc attendance patterns make it difficult for colleges to demonstrate their utility in terms of student outcomes, community college educators have begun to advocate a more directive approach to the college experience.

Miami-Dade Community College (Florida) provides a prominent example. Long before the current education reform movement took wing with the publication of *A Nation at Risk* in 1983, Miami-Dade instituted a number of reforms aimed at increasing and monitoring student progress (McCabe, 1981, 1983; Miami-Dade Community College, 1985). Among the initiatives was a matriculation process requiring English and mathematics placement testing for four categories of students: first-time students enrolling for nine or more credits; all students entering English or mathematics courses; all students who accumulate 15 or more credits; and all high school students concurrently enrolled in the college. In addition, the college established standards of academic progress used to monitor student performance, control the amount of credit for which students can enroll, and enforce regulations regarding academic probation and dismissal. These measures, along with a student information system that provides individualized feedback on mid-term academic performance and appraises students of their progress in meeting graduation and articulation requirements, combine high expectations for students with an institutional commitment to prescriptive counseling and support services. Direction is a key element, with student progress and achievement viewed as the necessary outcome of open-door policies. As McCabe (1981) explains, colleges should actively guide student enrollment and course-taking patterns:

> There should be a controlled student flow, carefully constructed so that students proceed through the program based on their competencies and progress. They should be enrolled in courses where they have a good chance to succeed. In a more directive system, students with deficiencies are required to take necessary developmental work before proceeding to programs where the lack of skill could cause failure. Such a system also ensures that students are assisted in selecting courses and in maintaining reasonable loads. Considerable effort is required to eliminate the problem of many students who work and carry a course load that is too great to permit the necessary study time. In addition, the curriculum should be aligned so that students that cannot complete a program will have gained skills and competencies that will be useful in their lives (p. 10).

Another signal example of reform is the California statewide matriculation plan. Like the Miami-Dade effort, the California plan, as it was originally developed, sought to replace ad hoc enrollment and attendance patterns with a more directed educational experience founded on six components:

- An admissions procedure that solicits information on the student's goals and special needs;

- Mandatory orientation for new students;

- Pre-enrollment testing, assessment, and counseling;

- Academic advisement;

- A computerized student tracking system to monitor student progress; and

- A comprehensive system of institutional research and evaluation to assess the plan's effectiveness (California Community Colleges, 1984).

While the system is still under development, it has done much to change the philosophy of open access, emphasizing that matriculation is an agreement between college and student and that both must pledge their best efforts toward the achievement of specified goals. Under the plan, matriculation is defined as:

> . . . a process which brings a college and a student who enrolls for credit into an agreement for the purpose of realizing the student's educational objective. The agreement acknowledges responsibilities of both parties to attain those objectives

through the college's established programs, policies, and requirements. On the college's part, the agreement includes providing an admissions process; an orientation to college programs, services, and procedures; pre-enrollment assessment and counseling; advisement and counseling for course selection; a suitable curriculum or program of courses; continuous follow-up on student progress with referral to support services when needed; and a program of institutional research and evaluation. On the student's part, the agreement includes expression of at least a broad educational intent at entrance and a willingness to declare a specific educational objective within a reasonable period of enrollment, diligence in class attendance and completion of assigned coursework, and completion of courses and maintenance of progress toward an educational goal according to standards established by the college and the State of California (Meznek and Murdoch, 1989, Appendix 3, p. 2).

In both the Miami-Dade and California examples, matriculation does not preclude students from taking a course or two on an ad hoc basis to upgrade job skills or fulfill personal interests. But the tighter matriculation philosophy recognizes that institutional approaches to these ad hoc students may not meet the needs of other individuals, particularly academically underprepared students seeking a certificate or associate degree as they advance through the educational pipeline. In response to the needs of these students, a bargain has been struck: colleges will provide the courses and support services necessary for success, and students will progress sequentially through the program, meeting all requirements. Central to this bargain is the assumption that colleges will identify those enrollees who can be considered matriculants, that is, students whose relationship with the college extends beyond simple enrollment and into the larger sphere of program or degree completion.

Research as a Corollary to Reform

Research into student flow and success has emerged as a corollary to tighter matriculation standards and, consequently, as a means of gauging institutional effectiveness. Indeed, outcomes assessment, though variously defined, generally links institutional evaluation to student success. Banta (1988), for example, highlights this linkage in the following definition:

> . . . outcomes assessment means collecting evidence of (1) student performance on specified measures of development, (2) program strengths and weaknesses, and (3) institutional effectiveness. By looking at what students and graduates know and are able to do with their knowledge, as well as at their perceptions of the quality of institutional programs and services, researchers can obtain important information about programs' ability to meet stated objectives for student development. The collective quality of its programs establishes the effectiveness of an institution (pp. 1-2).

The need for research along the lines outlined by Banta has been clearly articulated by state offices and accrediting agencies, which have mandated ambitious research agendas. In California, for example, institutional research is recognized as a key component of states' efforts to reform higher education:

> Institutional research is essential to determine which types of programs work best with which students under what circumstances, and to ensure the wisest use of public funds in meeting student and community needs. There is relatively little statewide institutional research available to evaluate the effectiveness of the Community College transfer, vocational, or remedial programs, which are of particular concern to this commission. If these programs are to be implemented successfully and cost-effectively, they must be accompanied by research and evaluation from the start, to strengthen these programs as they develop as well as to evaluate their ultimate merit. Significant additional funds will

be needed for this research (California Commission for the Review of the Master Plan for Higher Education, 1986, p. 12).

Virginia provides another example, with state regulations requiring each community college to develop a comprehensive student assessment plan encompassing evaluation of student performance and ability at several points of academic progression: entrance, mid-point through the program of study, graduation, and subsequently as employees or university transfers (Roesler, 1988). Outcomes research has also become a central part of the accreditation process, placing institutional effects, along with resources and processes, among the variables used to evaluate college quality. For example, the Commission on Colleges of the Southern Association of Colleges and Schools revised its standards in 1984 to include an "Institutional Effectiveness" criterion that stresses the college's responsibility to continually assess its effectiveness. In addition, the Southern Association stresses the importance of data collection and research, suggesting that institutions track changes in student academic achievement over time and establish and support institutional research programs (Moore, 1986, pp. 50-51).

With the political challenge of reform, then, comes the research challenge of accountability. State officials and accrediting agencies have made research on student progress a priority, augmenting ad hoc data reporting tasks with comprehensive research programs characterized by "visible, integrated, ongoing efforts governed by established policy and involving regular (and generally centralized) data collection and analysis" (Ewell, 1987a, p. 10). As a result, college practitioners have long ago accepted the "rhetoric of justification" and the "exhortations to get started" that characterized early discussions of the outcomes movement and are now looking for research models that can meet emerging information needs (Ewell, 1989, p. 1).

The challenge is particularly daunting for community colleges. The multiple goals of community college students make it difficult to gauge institutional effectiveness; standard measures of success, such as degree completion, are meaningless when only 10 percent of the students complete associate degrees or certificates. In addition, student outcomes that are basic to the community college mission, including transfer and employment, manifest themselves outside the domain of the community college, at the university or the workplace. The sheer magnitude of the research task poses another problem. Many community college personnel are hard-pressed enough to meet current data reporting requirements and have little experience in organizing the comprehensive research programs called for by state offices and accrediting agencies. While much has been written about the need for outcomes assessment, the more difficult question is how this assessment is to be implemented in practice at institutions that have diverse student populations and a limited research capacity.

Student Tracking Systems

In response to this research challenge, this monograph focuses on one of many promising research models: student tracking systems. The term "student tracking system" has been variously applied to any data collection or research effort aimed at gathering indicators of student success. For our purposes, however, a more precise definition will be used:

> *student tracking systems are longitudinal data bases that identify the attributes and educational goals of entering students, track student progress toward those goals on a term-by-term basis, and provide informational feedback for institutional planning and improvement.*

In keeping with the emerging matriculation plans, student tracking systems can help colleges tie outcomes to student intentions and attributes, thus yielding more precise indicators of student success.

Several factors should be considered in the development of a successful student tracking system. Long accustomed to the demands of state and federal data collection agencies that focus on cross-sectional data (such as fall enrollment and expenditures per student), some community colleges have relatively little experience conducting longitudinal analyses of student flow and outcomes. In addition, student tracking systems have inherent limitations; the data they yield, though useful indicators of student flow and progress, cannot of themselves meet the numerous information demands made by policy makers. (Indeed, some policy makers, as non-researchers, fail to draw a connection between the information they want and the effort required to secure that information.) Another problem stems from the fact that data in a student tracking system are usually drawn from different college offices, such as the registrar's office, the institutional research office, or even the data offices of neighboring four-year institutions (Moore, 1986, pp. 57-58). This dispersion usually requires an unprecedented degree of coordination and cooperation in the college's data collection effort. Finally, there is the problem of use; a student tracking system—however technically proficient—is not worth the investment if the data do not inform institutional planning and improvement. This is not to imply that tracking systems are exceptionally difficult to implement. On the contrary, much of the data needed for a tracking system are routinely collected by colleges already. The tracking system simply arrays the data in ways that make them more useful to those examining student flow and goal attainment. As Moore (1986) puts it: "A critical task for institutional researchers is the transformation of data into useful information" (p. 58).

This monograph is designed as a resource for the practitioner who may be considering the initiation of a community college student tracking system. Because the process of developing a tracking system involves broad questions of research methodology and not simply data processing skills, the monograph takes a conceptual approach, examining the construction and use of tracking systems within the overall framework of student flow analysis. Part Two reviews selected longitudinal and student flow studies that have been conducted at the national, state, and local levels. Part Three then considers the concept and interpretation of "indicators," data used in longitudinal and non-longitudinal studies as proxy measures for student success. Student tracking systems themselves are then considered in Part Four, which draws upon the literature and other sources to suggest models, note problems, and suggest solutions. The monograph concludes with two appendices, one outlining the components of the Texas LONESTAR student tracking system and one outlining the components of a closely related system suggested by a panel of experts convened by AACJC.

PART TWO:

THE SCOPE OF LONGITUDINAL RESEARCH AT COMMUNITY COLLEGES

THE SCOPE OF LONGITUDINAL RESEARCH AT COMMUNITY COLLEGES

Data collected on the nation's postsecondary institutions focus primarily on quantity, addressing the need for descriptive information on students, faculty, and finances. Accurate data on the number of colleges established, the number of students enrolled, the number of faculty and staff employed, expenditures per student, and other indicators of magnitude undergird fiscal accountability. Such data also provide benchmark measures of the growth of higher education since World War II.

But data collection efforts centering on simple description, although necessary, are not sufficient for understanding the broader accountability issues emerging in the 1980s and 1990s. College leaders are increasingly called upon to verify institutional effectiveness, particularly in the areas of student learning and goal attainment. Information related to student flow and outcomes must be added to the data on how many students are enrolled or how much is spent on instruction. Are students adequately prepared to continue their education, should they decide to do so? What do college graduates learn as a consequence of their undergraduate education? Does the college experience adequately prepare students for the workplace and for career mobility? Such questions—which are essential to telling the community college story—require data that provide longer-term assessments of institutional effects.

In addition, currently available data often grossly underestimate the effectiveness of community, technical, and junior colleges. For example, the number of associate degrees awarded is often used by the U.S. Department of Education as an indicator of postsecondary outcomes (see Baker and Ogle, 1989). This indicator has the advantage of being based on readily available information. But it says little about institutional effectiveness, because at community colleges (where 85 percent of all associate degrees are awarded) many students have no intention of earning an associate degree in the first place. Another problem area is transfer to four-year colleges and universities. When calculated by dividing the number of transfers by the number of students enrolled in community colleges, transfer rates appear shockingly low, in the area of 5 percent. Again, the problem lies in the denominator; many students have not enrolled with the intention of preparing for transfer. The lack of accurate data on student goals and the progression of students toward these goals leaves community colleges vulnerable to misperceptions about their effectiveness.

In the absence of accurate information on student flow, some attempts have been made to follow student cohorts longitudinally, tracing their progress over time through the community college and, in some cases, beyond. These studies are instructive to those building college-based student tracking systems, showing—among other things—the complex nature of student attendance patterns and the difficulties of capturing accurate baseline data (such as student educational intentions) that can be tied to outcomes in an effort to gauge institutional effectiveness.

National Longitudinal Studies

Several large-scale national studies have been undertaken or are currently underway to assess student flow through postsecondary education. Some of these studies are one-shot in nature, consisting of longitudinal analyses undertaken by individual researchers. Examples include the work of Borow and Hendrix (1974), who followed the progress (over a two-year period) of first-time, full-time students who attended 24 community colleges, and Wilms and Hansell (1982) who tracked the academic progress and employment success of community college and proprietary school students (both graduates and dropouts) in Chicago, San Francisco, Boston, and Miami. But because of the time required to track students longitudinally and because locating and surveying students at different points in time is expensive, most national longitudinal studies are conducted as part of larger, on-going research projects. One example is the Cooperative Institutional Research Program (CIRP), conducted jointly by the American Council on Education and UCLA's Higher Education Research Institute. CIRP researchers conduct an annual national survey of first-time college freshmen and occasionally follow up on the progress of these students to examine, among other topics, the factors that contribute to baccalaureate degree attainment (see, for example, Astin, 1977 and 1982). A second, more predominant example is the Postsecondary Longitudinal Studies Program of the U.S. Department of Education's National Center for Education Statistics (NCES). NCES longitudinal studies include, among others:

- The National Longitudinal Study of the High School Class of 1972 (NLS72), involving a national sample of high school seniors whose educational and employment experiences were tracked over a 14-year period (through 1986).

- The High School and Beyond Study (HSB), involving a national sample of high school sophomores and seniors in 1980 whose educational and employment histories have been tracked through mid-1986; and

- The Beginning Postsecondary Student (BPS) Longitudinal Study, which will follow, at two-year intervals, the educational progress and attainment of a national sample of students entering postsecondary education.

Regardless of type, the national studies are of no value in assessing institutional effectiveness *per se*; that is not their purpose. Dealing with national trends, the findings of these analyses speak to overall averages that apply to no institution in particular. Further, they are limited by their scope of coverage. All except the BPS Longitudinal Study focus on students entering college right after high school, a group that constitutes only about one-half of the community college student population. Indeed, NCES warns that its two largest studies conducted so far, the NLS72 and HSB analyses, are much more useful in assessing questions of college access and choice immediately following high school graduation than they are in addressing the issues of postsecondary educational attainment, access to graduate education, and the economic rate of return to education (National Center for Education Statistics, 1988, p. 4). The latter questions require longitudinal studies that go beyond the years immediately following high school, especially if one wants to capture the educational experiences of those who delay entry into college or of those who take a long period of time to attain a degree.

Nevertheless, the national studies represent ambitious attempts to change the focus of national data collection efforts from cross-sectional examinations of quantity to longitudinal analyses of student flow and attainment. In making this attempt, these studies have contributed greatly to our understanding of college-going patterns, patterns that are often more complex than is generally assumed, especially at community colleges. For example, Borow and Hendrix (1974) found that community college students in the late 1960s often changed majors, shifting from transfer to vocational programs and vice versa. The researchers concluded that while some students may be "cooled-out," switching from a collegiate to a career program, others appear to switch in the opposite direction and are thus "warmed up," a phenomenon often ignored by community college critics. As another example, the HSB has demonstrated that the traditional pattern of college attendance, four years of full-time study culminating in the baccalaureate, applies only to a minority of American youths. For every 1,000 high school graduates in 1980, only 157 (16 percent) followed this traditional pattern toward the baccalaureate immediately after high school (Carroll, 1989, p. 11). Many students delayed their entry into college and followed a more sporadic pattern of attendance, enrolling on a part-time, infrequent basis.

Another factor illuminated by the national studies is the correlation between student plans for education after high school and eventual educational attainment. For example, in the NLS 72 study, high school seniors in 1972 were asked to state the type of education they would most likely pursue: no postsecondary education (high school only); vocational/technical college; two-year college; four-year college; or advanced degree. As Figure One illustrates, students' answers to this question were generally associated with educational attainment 14 years later: students aspiring to advanced degrees were more likely to attain them; students who did not plan to go to college were less likely to attain higher degrees.

These observations concerning course-taking patterns and the link between goals and attainment demonstrate the power longitudinal studies have to describe student behavior and, to some degree, outcomes. But experience with the national studies also illustrates the problems that crop up when data are used to attempt explanations of these behaviors. In some cases the explanations offered by researchers have centered on the relative efficiency of different sectors of higher education, usually comparing community colleges with four-year institutions. For example, Carroll (1989) used the HSB data to compare the baccalaureate attainment rates (as of 1986) of two groups of 1980 high school graduates: (1) "on-track" students who began full-time studies at a four-year college immediately after high school graduation; and (2) "off-track" students who began postsecondary studies at a community college, who delayed entry into college, or who attended part-time. Noting that the baccalaureate attainment rate of the former group was higher than the rate of the latter, the researchers warn of the inefficiency of nontraditional enrollment patterns, concluding that, "Beyond the obvious impact of a decision never to attend a postsecondary institution, the other paths through postsecondary education [including attending a two-year college] drastically affect the likehood of eventually attaining a bachelor's degree" (Carroll, 1989, p. 29). Admitting that high school students may not have control over which paths to follow or that "there may be moderating characteristics that render the track model meaningless, " the researchers nonetheless warn that "off-track" students pursue an inefficient path: ". . . in times of scarce resources for the provision of opportunities and services, efficiency from the point of view of the institution may be an important issue" (Carroll, 1989, p.30).

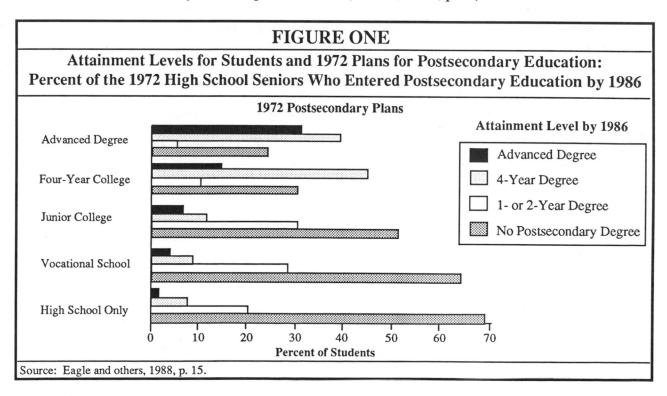

FIGURE ONE

Attainment Levels for Students and 1972 Plans for Postsecondary Education: Percent of the 1972 High School Seniors Who Entered Postsecondary Education by 1986

1972 Postsecondary Plans

Attainment Level by 1986

■ Advanced Degree
▨ 4-Year Degree
□ 1- or 2-Year Degree
▨ No Postsecondary Degree

Percent of Students

Source: Eagle and others, 1988, p. 15.

Another example can be found in Astin's analyses of CIRP data, which led him to conclude that—after controlling for socioeconomic status, educational aspiration, high school background, and other pertinent variables—students who begin their studies at a community college are less likely to attain a baccalaureate than students who begin their studies at a four-year institution. Among the reasons for this, he concludes, is the nontraditional structure of the community college, which caters to the part-time, commuting students and has few of the characteristics that are highly correlated with baccalaureate degree attainment, such as opportunities for on-campus residence, for involvement in campus life through involvement in on-campus jobs and extracurricular activities, or full-time study. He concludes that the economic efficiency of community colleges, usually characterized as low-cost institutions, is misleading and argues that policy makers wishing to expand educational opportunity to students from low socioeconomic backgrounds should consider other alternatives besides the expansion of community college systems: "Although community colleges are generally less expensive to construct and operate than four-year colleges, their 'economy' may be somewhat illusory, particularly when measured in terms of the cost of producing each baccalaureate recipient" (Astin, 1977, p. 255).

The hypothesis that community colleges are an inefficient avenue to the baccalaureate has been challenged by some who question the underlying assumptions of the methodology used by Astin and other researchers who compare the educational attainment of students beginning college at four-year and two-year institutions. For example, Cohen and Brawer (1989) argue that Astin's analysis makes the implicit assumption that all students have a choice between a two-year college and a four-year institution. In fact, Cohen and Brawer continue, many students are faced with the choice of a community college or no college at all; thus, the community college may greatly enhance the likelihood of baccalaureate attainment. Another point of contention about Astin's hypothesis is the question used in the CIRP studies to assess educational aspirations and hence measure the degree to which students meet educational goals: "What is the highest academic degree that you intend to obtain?" Lopsided majorities of the community college respondents indicate that they want to earn a baccalaureate or higher, suggesting that transfer rates to four-year institutions are nowhere near as high as they should be. Brawer (1988) argues that this is a hypothetical question that is unconnected to the student's immediate intentions and leads to exaggerated notions of student educational goals. She suggests another question: "What is your most important reason for attending this college at this time? (choose one):

- To prepare for transfer to a four-year college or university;

- To gain skills necessary to enter a new occupation;

- To gain skills necessary to retrain, remain concurrent, or advance in a concurrent occupation;

- To satisfy a personal interest."

Citing student surveys undertaken by the Center for the Study of Community Colleges, she shows that while 60 to 75 percent of the community college students say they plan to earn a baccalaureate, only 35 percent indicate that they have enrolled to prepare for transfer to a four-year college or university. Thus, those concluding that community colleges are a relatively inefficient vehicle of educational attainment may be drawing logical conclusions from questionable data.

Longitudinal studies, like other research models, pose problems of interpretation. Those building student tracking systems need to realize that the questions they ask in student surveys are as important as the technical concerns related to data input and processing. Student answers to different questions, when correlated with outcomes, will yield different interpretations of institutional effectiveness.

Experience with available longitudinal studies conducted at the national level demonstrates that researchers need to know the limitations of the data that are used.

State Longitudinal Studies

States are key players in higher education data collection and are expressing a growing interest in improved information on student flow and success. In California, for example, the state assembly directed the California Postsecondary Education Commission (CPEC) to "develop a feasibility plan for a study to provide comprehensive information about factors which affect students' progress through California's educational system, from elementary school through postgraduate education" (California Education Code, Chapter 4, Section 99172). The CPEC plan proposed an ambitious "modified longitudinal study" using samples of students at different points in the educational pipeline. Going far beyond the usual questions of how many students are enrolled and how many degrees are awarded, the proposed study would assess access to education, student progress through the educational pipeline, and subsequent student success in the job market. Comparisons for ethnicity, gender, and socioeconomic status were to be made throughout. The enormity of the task is made clear in the study proposal. The project, it points out, would:

> initiate data collection at several educational levels concurrently and then follow each set of students through the education system and on to work at least until their progress overlaps that of the student groups one level above theirs. .... The academic record of the student in the first sampling year would provide basic demographic information, such as sex, ethnicity, birth date, as well as academic courses taken with grades earned, test scores, and participation in supplementary educational programs, and institutional characteristics. This information would be updated annually with information from the institution of current enrollment. These data would need to be supplemented by information not routinely available, such as students' or former students' social and economic circumstances .... To gather the facts on individuals" circumstances, annual or biennial surveys of students, former students, and/or their parents or guardians would be required to track changes in their conditions, aspirations, and non-academic achievements. (California Postsecondary Education Commission, 1986, pp. 3-4).

Few state efforts are as ambitious as this plan for comprehensive student information. Cost is no small obstacle. Indeed, initial estimates indicated that the California plan would incur direct costs of approximately $2 million plus an additional $100 million to modify existing data collection systems at individual colleges and schools (California Postsecondary Education Commission, 1986, p. 4). These modifications point to another problem: the uneven research capacity of individual colleges, where data collection efforts are ultimately carried out, regardless of where the mandate for such studies emanates. CPEC factored this unevenness in its data collection plan:

> As is the case for elementary and secondary school districts, the quality of the Chancellor's Office data bases depends on the reporting capabilities of the local Community College districts. Districts vary widely in the nature and capabilities of their computer facilities, and some small districts with no computing capabilities submit their reports to the Chancellor's Office in hard copy only. The resulting incompatability requires adjustments by the Chancellor's Office that can interfere with timely reporting. Other disruptions in reporting may occur when districts change computer hardware or upgrade their existing facilities. (California Postsecondary Education Commission, 1986, p. 15).

Just as those building college student tracking systems face the task of organizing data from different campus offices with sometimes incompatible computer equipment, state offices must gather information from campuses using different data collection and processing techniques. Another problem is data coding and the difficulty of assuring that student records are tagged with a common identification number, which allows for the merger of student records at different institutions, such as community colleges and neighboring four-year institutions (Alkin, 1985). Nonetheless,these problems are being addressed, and statewide information on student flow and progress may become more available in the future. Since the 1986 CPEC proposal, for example, California has made great strides in developing a statewide management information system that will, among other things, link student demographic data with course data, thus allowing policy makers to track student progress over time (Hamre and Holsclaw, 1989). Other examples of statewide longitudinal studies that have appeared in the literature are briefly noted below.

California Statewide Longitudinal Study

In a four-year longitudinal study of 6,500 first-time students entering 15 California community colleges in fall 1978, Sheldon (1982) attempted to classify student educational goals and trace student progress toward those goals. His findings belie the simplistic but popular notion of the community college as an institution with separate curricular tracks for three student types: vocational students preparing for entry into the labor market; transfer students preparing for upper-division studies at four-year colleges or universities; and other adult students pursuing special interests that do not require a credential. In fact, Sheldon identified 18 student prototypes, outlined in Figure Two, showing that students come to the community college with a variety of objectives. Sheldon also demonstrated that curriculum content is independent of student intent. A student's decision to enroll in an occupational program, for example, does not always mean that the student will not transfer. As Cohen and Brawer (1987) observed:

> The California Statewide Longitudinal Study showed more than one-fourth of the students enrolled in occupational programs indicating that they intended to transfer, and more than one-fourth of the students enrolled in transfer credit classes indicating that they were attending college to gain job-related skills (p. 96).

Along with these insights, however, the California Statewide Longitudinal Study points to a potentially troublesome aspect of student tracking research: the temptation to investigate all permutations of student types, comparing the progress and attainment of students classified along numerous variables. Student tracking systems array data in such a way that any number of student cohorts can be identified for analysis. But at the institutional level, the 18 cohort groups or "prototypes" investigated by Sheldon may prove an unmanageable framework, requiring numerous cells that include too few students for meaningful comparison and analysis. The problem is compounded when ethnicity, gender, and other demographic variables are taken into consideration. The challenge, then, is to balance the need to identify and compare student groups exhibiting distinct behavioral patterns with the limited research capacity of the college. This is a difficult task at the community college with its diverse student body and with the numerous course-taking patterns that emerge. (For a discussion of the difficulties of using a tracking system to identify student behavioral patterns, see Bers and Rubin, 1989.)

Illinois

The Illinois Community College Board (ICCB) has conducted several statewide longitudinal studies. Examples include the Statewide Occupational Student Follow-Up Study, involving a four-year

FIGURE TWO

Student Prototypes Identified by the
California Statewide Longitudinal Study, 1978-1982

1. **The Full-Time Transfers** (10.6%) represent both those who are eligible for the university from high school and those who just missed eligibility.

2. **The Part-Time Transfers** (7.7%) are older than the full-time students and enroll in three or fewer courses, usually in the evening.

3. **The Undisciplined Transfers** (9.3%) aspire to transfer, but have a low probability of their doing so. They lack either the academic skills to complete their work or the self-discipline to follow through on their studies and homework.

4. **The Technical Transfers** (7.7%) are indistinguishable from the full-time or part-time transfer students other than that they enroll in, and complete, a sequence of courses in a high-level vocational area.

5. **The Intercollegiate Athletes** (0.7%) are indistinguishable from the Undisciplined Transfer Students other than their prime motive for attendance--athletics.

6. **The Financial Support Seekers** (0.3%) are also indistinguishable from the Undisciplined Transfer Students who attend to get financial aid.

7. **The Expediters'** (0.7%) main academic affiliation is with a senior college but find it convenient to take some courses at the community college.

8. **The Program Completers** (5.7%) enroll in, and expect to complete, a vocational program.

9. **The Job Seekers** (13.5%) attend college only to learn enough to obtain a semi-skilled job.

10. **The Job-Upgraders** (12.3%) are already employed in the field in which they take courses and attend classes to improve their present skills or learn new complementary skills.

11. **The Career Changers** (3.3%) are employed but wish to learn new job skills to change careers or to supplement their incomes by "moonlighting."

12. **The License Maintainers** (0.7%) are in careers that necessitate state licensing and require instruction on a regular basis to maintain the license.

13. **The Leisure Skills Students** (12.4%) are concerned with learning specific skills to pursue their hobbies. The courses they take are vocational, individual sports, or artistic performance.

14. **The Education Seekers** (6.3%) feel a vague discomfort or guilt if they are not enrolled in a reasonably academic course.

15. **The Art and Culture Students** (1.0%) seek cultural experiences in courses such as art or music appreciation, or humanities that may include attendance at concerts.

16. **The Explorer/Experimenters** (4.0%) attend community colleges primarily to study themselves and explore avenues of potential employment or a continuation of their education.

17. **Basic Skills Students** (2.9%) attend a college to improve basic skills. Many are recent immigrants whose goal is to learn or improve their English.

18. **Lateral Transfers** (0.8%) are taking courses prior to transferring to an institution other than a university for a vocational program.

Source: Sheldon and Grafton, 1982, pp. 19-20. (Percentages refer to the percent of students in each prototype.)

longitudinal analysis of students entering community college occupational programs in fall 1974 (ICCB, 1979), and the Illinois Community College Board Transfer Study, a five-year longitudinal analysis conducted to follow the progress of 9,757 students who transferred to Illinois senior colleges and universities in fall 1979 (ICCB, 1986). These studies, like the Sheldon analysis in California, confirm that community college students are a diverse group whose goals and attendance patterns do not always follow institutional prescriptions. The Statewide Occupational Student Follow-Up Study, for example, found that only 56 percent of the state's vocational students had enrolled with the intention of preparing for employment in new career areas (many, in fact, were already employed in jobs related to their studies) and that many students enrolled with objectives that could be met by completing as few as one or two courses. The transfer study also found a great deal of diversity; 62 percent of the students transferring to four-year colleges did so without completing an associate degree, and 56 percent of the transfers had earned fewer than 60 credits at the community college. This pattern of transfer runs counter to the Illinois Transfer Compact, which ties articulation and credit transfer to completion of the associate degree (ICCB, 1989). In addition, the study between two- and four-year institutions also found that students who transfer after completing the associate degree tend to have better academic records at the university than those who transfer after completing only a few credits at the community college.

The Illinois studies demonstrate that, with appropriate leadership at the state level, student performance data recorded in the files of various colleges can be merged and analyzed to draw pictures of student flow and progress. The task faced by the ICCB in conducting these studies was not to collect new data, but to make use of existing data in student transcripts and, in the case of the vocational study, occupational follow-up surveys of vocational students. Thus, the Illinois data derive from secondary analyses of college files and are reliable to the extent that individual colleges collect accurate information. In the case of term-by-term student transcripts, this does not appear to be a problem. But follow-up surveys are another matter, with great variation in results between colleges. In another 1979 study, for example, the ICCB drew upon follow-up surveys conducted by each of the state's community colleges to examine the employment and educational status of 7,773 students who graduated from occupational programs in 1978. The statewide response rate was 53 percent, but individual college response rates varied from 26 to 92 percent (Lach and others, 1979). This variation illustrates the difficulty colleges have in gathering follow-up information and tying it with transcript data to develop tracking systems that extend beyond college attendance.

Kansas

Johnson County Community College in Overland Park, Kansas, has played a central role in initiating and coordinating longitudinal studies of the state's community college students. For example, Doucette and Teeter (1985) describe a 1984 study examining student mobility between the 19 community colleges and six state universities in Kansas. The study was conducted cooperatively between those institutions and involved three components: (1) coordinated analyses of student data bases at the universities to determine the demographic and academic characteristics of community college transfer students entering the universities from fall 1979 through spring 1984; (2) a survey of former community college students enrolled in these universities in fall 1984; and (3) a retrospective longitudinal examination of selected groups of native university and community college transfer students. The findings revealed mixed results, indicating that the academic performance of community college transfers was substantially the same as native university students, although the persistence of former community college students toward the baccalaureate was somewhat lower. Doucette and Teeter warn of study limitations, however, created by "data definitions and differences in the student information data bases at the six universities." The need to compromise on an operational definition of "transfer student," for example, led to the following most-common-denominator: "any student enrolled in a state university and who listed a Kansas Community College as the 'institution last attended' on admissions/registration material" (p. 10). As a result, the study sample included a wide spectrum of students, including those who had completed only one course at the community college as well as those who had completed a full associate degree program. In addition, "the definition excluded students who may have had considerable community college experience but who had intervening experience at another college or university" (p. 10).

In a second cooperative study coordinated by Johnson County Community College, limitations of another sort cropped up. The study began in fall 1985, when each of the 19 public community colleges in Kansas randomly selected 50 to 100 first-time, full-time freshmen who agreed in writing to complete an initial survey and cooperate with researchers who would conduct subsequent follow-up surveys over the next five years to monitor the students' progress toward their educational and career goals. Some colleges were more successful than others, however, in conducting the follow-up surveys and forwarding the data to Johnson County for analysis. For example, only 12 of the 19 colleges provided information on the fall 1987 follow-up survey, thus severely limiting the data reported in the study's two-year interim report (Johnson County Community College, 1987). Here, again, is an example of how the uneven research capacity and commitment of individual institutions makes statewide studies difficult to conduct.

Wyoming

The Wyoming Community College Commission initiated a five-year longitudinal study in fall 1987 to determine the variables that affect student progress toward personal, academic, and career objectives. Being a sparsely populated state with relatively low community college enrollments, the sample consisted of only 181 randomly selected, first-time, first-year students attending one of Wyoming's seven public community colleges. An initial survey was conducted in October 1987 to develop a profile of the students and identify their educational and career goals. Follow-up surveys are being conducted at six-month intervals. As of this writing, only the results of the initial survey and the first follow-up are available (Kitchens, 1987; Wyoming Community College Commission, 1988).

Problems in Statewide Studies

While many states collect student follow-up data gathered by individual colleges--and thus provide some statewide measure of transfer, graduate job placement, and other student outcomes--most states have not followed through on their demands for improved information on student success with the requisite support for rigorous longitudinal research. The literature yields few statewide longitudinal studies, and those that do exist are often limited by the uneven research capacity of individual colleges, by differing data base configurations and definitions used by the colleges, and by the sheer magnitude of the task (especially in collecting follow-up information after students leave the college). States can do little to improve the picture of student flow and outcomes as long as individual colleges are unable or unwilling to collect the requisite data.

In the face of these difficulties, some states are beginning to assist colleges with the research effort itself rather than simply mandating that certain data be collected. One approach is to provide colleges with data processing assistance. For example, researchers in California have worked on a microcomputer-based software package that is tied to standardized classroom and follow-up questionnaires used in gathering data on student flow through vocational programs and job attainment afterwards. The software package, which is compatible with most of the microcomputers used by the state's community colleges, allows administrators with limited computer expertise to disaggregate data collected in student follow-up surveys by the initial goals of students, as determined by classroom surveys. It would be possible, for example, to determine the job placement rates of those students who enrolled in vocational programs with the intention of preparing for a new career. (Figure Three provides an example of such a cross-tabulation.) The state hopes this assistance will improve data on vocational programs. As Farland, Anderson, and Boakes (1987) explain:

> A review of the status of student follow-up revealed that, despite the widespread interest in assessment and placement, only a few of the 106 California community colleges have the resources to conduct extensive follow-up on students. And, as might be expected, locally developed student follow-up systems tend to be quite different from one another, which detracts from any meaningful aggregation of data. The introduction by the federal government of the Vocational Education Data System (VEDS) in 1976 locked colleges into a set of required procedures. Since that time, colleges have gone through the motions of conducting a follow-up study of their former vocational students every year. In many instances, however, these studies have amounted to sending double postcards containing the compulsory questions to an undefined group of students and receiving a low response rate. The responses have typically been aggregated by class, by college, by district, and finally by state, with each aggregation further diluting the hope for meaningful findings (p. 3).

Besides data processing assistance, more complex efforts have been undertaken to improve data collection at the institutional level. One approach is to provide colleges with uniform questionnaires that can be processed at a central location, thus relieving the colleges of the task of designing survey instruments, coding the responses, and keying in the data. Examples of such comprehensive efforts include the Michigan Student Information System (MiSIS) and the Texas Student Information System (TEX-SIS). A third approach is to provide colleges with computer assistance *and* expert advice on how to collect requisite data. The Texas LONESTAR student tracking system, discussed in Part Four of this monograph, is an example, combining a software program with a guidebook describing the methodology involved in establishing and maintaining a longitudinal data base.

FIGURE THREE

Sample Status Report for Electronics Students, Utilizing Software Developed by California Statewide Student Follow-up Project

TOP: 093400 Electronic/Electrical Tech	Total Students in 1984-85	Still in College in 1985-86		Employed in 1985-86		Unemployed in 1985-86		
		Same College	Another College	Job is Related	Job Not Related	Seeking Work	Not Seeking	Status Unknown
Prepare for a New Career	1,124	389	15	72	34	13	4	597
Prepare for a Job Change	458	142	3	61	9	0	0	243
Improve Skill at the Present Job	362	109	0	60	10	1	0	182
Maintain a License	57	22	1	1	0	3	0	30
Totals	2,001	662	19	194	53	17	4	1,052

Employment Percentages	Total Job Market			Job is Related	Job Not Related	Seeking Work		
Prepare for a New Career	119			0.60	0.28	0.10		
Prepare for a Job Change	70			0.87	0.12	0.00		
Improve Skill at the Present Job	71			0.84	0.14	0.01		
Maintain a License	4			0.25	0.08	0.75		
Totals	264			0.73	0.20	0.06		

1. At the top of the page, student's primary purpose for attending classes as recorded during the 1984-85 Classroom Survey is cross-tabulated with the student's employment or college status recorded one year later.
2. At the bottom of the page, the job status of students who were known to have entered the job market is expressed as a percentage of the number of students in the three job market categories.

Source: Farland, Anderson, and Boakes, 1987, p. A-11.

College-Based Longitudinal Studies

Community colleges have always gathered information on their students. Follow-up studies, particularly of vocational students, are common practice and have provided at least a sporadic picture of the success of associate degree graduates (Palmer, 1985). Surveys of the goals of entering students are also common. Recent examples include goal analyses from the Community College of Philadelphia (1987), Glendale Community College in Arizona (Montemayor and others, 1985), Kirkwood Community College in Iowa (Koefoed, 1985), the San Francisco Community College District (Moss, 1985), and Broome Community College in New York (Romano, 1985). Both the follow-up studies and the goal analyses provide at least some indicators of student characteristics at entry and at exit. When these studies and analyses are collected routinely on an annual basis, valuable trend data or indicators can emerge. For example, if over time there is an increase in the proportion of entering students who enroll with the intention of transferring, follow-up studies might find a corresponding rise in the proportion of graduates or leavers who enroll in four-year institutions. Few colleges, however, have made longitudinal analyses a routine part of their institutional research effort. Unlike cross-sectional studies, in which a student cohort is examined at a single point in time, longitudinal studies examine student cohorts progressively over a specified period of time. While ad hoc longitudinal studies of special populations occasionally appear, reports generated from comprehensive longitudinal data bases are rarely found in the literature. Those studies that do exist usually track student persistence through the institution without looking at outcomes after graduation (or leaving) or without drawing a link between outcomes and student goals. Examples of studies available in the literature are described below.

Miami-Dade Community College (Florida)

Miami-Dade Community College often draws upon its student information systems to track the progress of entering student cohorts, particularly for special populations. For example, the college's office of institutional research has examined the longitudinal progress of students enrolled in English-as-a-Second-Language courses (Belcher, 1988), as well as the subsequent progress of dual enrollment students who are enrolled simultaneously in the college and in surrounding high schools (Baldwin, 1988). Such studies are an attempt to disaggregate the enrollment patterns and attainment rates of different student groups.

Underlying the studies is Miami-Dade's commitment to the development of student success indicators that bespeak the community college's nontraditional student body. In one longitudinal study, for example, Morris and Losak (1986) illustrate the use of these measures, tracking the three-year progress of full-time, degree-seeking students entering Miami-Dade each fall from fall 1977 through fall 1982. Arguing that the use of degree completion as a sole success measure reflects outdated thinking about student college-going behavior, Morris and Losak assert that students can be considered successful if they remain in good academic standing during their tenure at college, regardless of whether they receive a degree. Thus, at any one point and time, a student can be considered "successful" if he or she (1) has graduated, (2) is still enrolled in good academic standing, or (3) has left college in good academic standing. (See Figure Four).

FIGURE FOUR			
Suggested Student Outcome Categories, Miami-Dade Community College			
Academic Standing	Graduated	Still Enrolled	Left College
GPA $\geq$ 2.00	(1) Success	(2) Success	(3) Success
GPA $\geq$ 2.00	(4) n/a	(5) Non-Success	(6) Non-Success
Source: Morris and Losak, 1986, p. 7.			

Using this methodology, the Miami-Dade researchers were able to show total success rates for each cohort of approximately 65 percent. For example, of the cohort of degree-seeking students entering Miami-Dade in 1982, 19 percent graduated within three years, 20 percent were still enrolled in good standing, and 26 percent left the college while in good standing. (See Table One.)

If the associate degree is irrelevant to large numbers of students who use community colleges for their own purposes without completing a full program of study, then these data may provide an accurate picture of student success. But the Miami-Dade study points again to the problem of interpretation and the need to articulate the underlying assumptions of the methodology used in longitudinal analyses. The student success measures used by Morris and Losak represent a compromise, "selected so as to avoid self-serving definitions on the one hand, or inherently devastating measures on the other. The authors believe that those [measures] selected represent an optional synthesis rooted in institutional mission and reality-based student behavior" (Morris and Losak, 1986, p. 16). The need to identify appropriate outcomes measures that gauge institutional effectiveness without being self-serving is one of the major challenges facing those designing longitudinal studies of student flow and persistence.

TABLE ONE				
Three-Year Success Rates for Students Beginning As Full-Time Degree Seekers* Miami-Dade Community College				
Beginning Fall Term	Percentage Graduated	Percentage Still Enrolled in Good Standing	Percentage Who Left College in Good Standing	Total Percentage Success
1977	25%	11	27	64
1978	28	12	27	67
1979	33	11	25	69
1980	28	13	27	68
1981	28	15	26	69
1982	19	20	26	64
1983	19	26	19	64
1984	17	26	19	62
1985	18	28	18	64
*Registered for 12 or more credits during their first term, and showed program and matriculation codes of degree seeking.				
Source: Morris and Losak, 1986, p. 9.; unpublished data supplied by Miami-Dade Community College.				

William Rainey Harper College (Illinois)

The ERIC files include several longitudinal studies conducted at William Rainey Harper College (WRHC) to assess the progress of entering student cohorts. As an example, Lucas (1986) analyzed the transcripts from random samples of 200 full-time and 200 part-time students entering WRHC in successive classes between 1974 and 1984. The study yielded trend data on several indicators of persistence and success, including cumulative hours attempted versus cumulative hours passed, the percent of students who never returned after the first year, and the average number of semesters for which students registered. The WRHC data illustrate the wide variety of enrollment patterns exhibited by community college students, even those who enrolled on a full-time basis. While approximately 20 percent of the full-time students never returned after the first year of enrollment, another 50 percent spread out their enrollment over a long period of time (five or more semesters). Table Two details these findings, showing that much can be done through a careful analysis of enrollment data that are usually part of the student's transcript.

TABLE TWO
Longitudinal Data of Full-time Degree Credit Students at William Rainey Harper College

Students Beginning in the Fall of:

	1974	1975	1976	1977	1978	1979	1980	1981	1982	1983	1984
Sample Size	200	200	200	200	200	200	200	200	200	200	200
Mean GPA	2.60	2.63	2.64	2.64	2.68	2.58	2.56	2.58	2.20	2.45	2.48
Mean Cumulative Hours Attempted	46.98	44.06	44.26	46.38	47.75	46.39	49.58	45.77	42.60	39.96	25.99
Mean Cumulative Hours Passed	46.05	43.10	42.93	45.32	47.10	45.38	47.16	43.58	38.82	37.73	24.68
Percent Registered 1 Year Later	68.5	60.0	59.5	60.5	65.0	65.0	68.0	67.0	70.5	65.0	69.5
Percent Not Registered 1 Year Later but who Return Another Time	13.5	14.5	16.0	16.0	12.0	12.0	15.5	9.0	11.0	9.5	0
Percent who Never Return After First Year	18.0	25.5	24.5	23.5	23.0	23.0	16.5	24.0	18.5	25.5	30.5
Average Number of Semesters Registered	5.0	4.6	4.7	4.8	4.9	4.7	5.0	4.7	4.4	3.8	2.2
Percent Registering for:											
One Semester	4.5	7.0	4.5	4.5	6.0	5.5	4.5	3.5	8.0	5.5	8.5
Two Semesters	15.5	18.0	17.0	17.0	16.0	16.0	9.0	19.0	12.5	19.0	66.0
Three Semesters	9.5	13.0	17.0	13.5	7.5	10.5	12.0	11.0	15.0	12.0	25.5
Four Semesters	20.5	14.5	14.5	15.0	15.0	16.0	18.5	14.0	15.0	33.0	0
Five Semesters	14.0	17.0	18.5	16.0	18.5	20.0	14.0	19.5	13.0	17.5	0
Six Semesters	13.5	13.5	10.0	11.5	14.0	12.5	17.5	14.0	20.5	13.0	0
Seven or More Semesters	22.5	17.0	18.5	22.5	23.0	19.5	24.5	19.0	16.0	0	0

Source: Lucas, 1986, pp. 8-9.

Mercer County Community College (New Jersey)

At Mercer County Community College (MCCC), a study was undertaken in 1985 to assess the educational progress of 1,532 full-time students who entered the college in fall 1980. Utilizing both an analysis of the students' transcripts and responses to a 1984 follow-up survey of the students, the goal of the study was to distinguish the educational and career outcomes of graduates from those of non-graduates. Included in the analysis were 240 non-returners who attended for only one semester, 652 non-graduates who attended for two or more consecutive semesters, 237 stop-outs who attended intermittently, and 403 graduates as of spring 1984. The study allowed the college to compare graduation rates between programs, determine the extent to which graduates and non-graduates attended another college after leaving MCCC, and compare the employment experiences of graduates and non-graduates. In addition the follow-up survey questionnaire asked respondents to indicate their primary goal when they first entered the college, thus providing the opportunity to link, however roughly, initial goals with actual outcomes.

Among other findings, the college determined that graduates were more likely to be employed while attending MCCC (83 percent) than non-returners (49 percent). Students who were not employed tended to leave school once they secured a job, thus suggesting that for many students program completion may be irrelevant; they attend college for only as long as it takes to find employment. The MCCC study, detailed by Edwards and Staatse (1985), thus illustrates the use of transcript data and follow-up surveys in making inferences about student motives and the factors that affect enrollment decisions.

Community College of Philadelphia

Earlier in the decade, the Community College of Philadelphia (CCP) (1982) analyzed the transcripts of 893 students who graduated from the college in 1982 in order to analyze their attendance patterns. Starting in fall 1974, these students were tracked, with particular attention given to the number of semesters enrolled, credit hours earned, and indicators of academic difficulties, stop-out behavior, and curriculum changes. The study determined that most students did not earn a degree within two years; 46 percent took over three years to graduate and 30 percent stopped out for at least one semester between initial enrollment and graduation. Additional analyses were undertaken to examine the reasons students had for stopping in and out and to examine the extent to which students changed curricula. Noting that stop-outs did not have significantly lower grade point averages than those who followed an uninterrupted pattern of study, it was reasoned that personal, rather than academic problems led to stop-out behavior. As for curricular changes, course-taking patterns revealed that up to 24 percent of the students enrolled during any one semester changed their program of study, usually moving into and out of the college's general studies program. There was no noticeable movement between collegiate and career programs. "When programs other than General Studies were involved in changes, in the majority of cases they were within the same division, i.e., change from Secretarial Science to Office Science" (Community College of Philadelphia, 1982, p. 13).

The transcript analysis again demonstrates that researchers can use readily available student information to gain insights into student behavior without resorting to special surveys. The key lies in arraying and interpreting data so that they yield information. More recently, CCP designed a comprehensive "Retention Data Base" providing demographic, personal background, and academic data on every student who entered the college in the eight years prior to 1987. With the data base, the college now has the capacity to link outcomes data collected in follow-up surveys to demographic and academic information stored in college files. As Hawk (1987) explains:

> The file makes it possible for us to load a rich set of variables for all respondents to survey research so that we look at the relationships between entering goals, race, sex, SES, remedial program status, etc., and post-CCP outcomes. This is important to us because of the increasing emphasis we are placing on why something happened as opposed to just what happened (p. 11).

Longitudinal Studies: Conclusion

It is one thing to ask "How many students were enrolled in fall 1986?", quite another to ask "What happened to these students during the past three years?" Longitudinal analyses of student flow, whether they are conducted retrospectively through an examination of student transcripts or (more rarely) progressively through a sequential term-by-term analysis of student progress, pose a more formidable research task than cross-sectional analyses. To date, the most extensive longitudinal studies have been conducted at the national level, with community college students included among other subjects in large-scale research projects examining the educational and employment experiences of youths immediately out of high school. And, ironically, it is at the national level—far removed from the playing field of institutional policy making—that longitudinal studies have been most often used to make judgments about the effectiveness of the community college. Where state or local studies are available, they are usually analyses of student transcript data conducted on an ad hoc basis to examine cohort enrollment and survival patterns. These studies provide valuable insights into student course-taking behavior, but they are anomalies in the world of institutional research.

The dearth of state and locally based longitudinal studies in the literature points to a potentially large gap between the information demands of policy makers on the one hand and the research capacity of community colleges on the other. While accrediting agencies and state higher education offices increasingly link institutional accountability to data documenting student persistence and success, policy makers have rarely drawn the connection between the information they want and the research effort that will be required to gather that information. If today's outcomes assessment movement is to become a permanent fixture in practice, college researchers will need the wherewithal and expertise required to conduct longitudinal analyses of student progress toward their educational goals. Technical assistance in the form of centrally administered student information systems (such as the Michigan Student Information System) or in the form of specially developed data analysis software are steps in the right direction.

But besides this assistance, steps may need to be taken to limit the scope of longitudinal analyses, making them feasible within the considerable budgetary constraints under which community college reseachers operate. One way to make longitudinal studies more manageable is to specify in advance what data, or "indicators," the college's longitudinal data base will yield. While there is a temptation to measure student flow against any number of academic, demographic, or socioeconomic variables, limitations in financial resources and staff time may dictate that only selected variables be examined. The process of building a tracking system, then, ideally begins with the question "What indicators of student flow will we use to assess college effectiveness?" As the Morris and Losak (1986) study at Miami-Dade Community College indicates, the selection of these indicators is a difficult process, requiring researchers to specify variables that yield accurate indicators of student success without presenting an exaggerated and self-serving picture of the institution.The next section of the monograph examines efforts previously undertaken to identify such indicators and discusses problems in their use as measures of institutional effectiveness.

PART THREE:

INDICATORS OF
INSTITUTIONAL EFFECTIVENESS

INDICATORS OF INSTITUTIONAL EFFECTIVENESS

The outcomes assessment movement, though a child of the 1980s, has deep roots in the history of the modern community college. As Simmons (1988) explains, efficiency reforms are not new.

> Other movements, particularly in the last 25 years, have either been developed fully or have been adopted and pursued fervently by the community college. Whether one examines the systems approach, behavioral objectives, cognitive style mapping, mastery learning, management by objectives (MBO), or strategic planning, the common thread for the community college sector has been its responsiveness and often proactive stance—to change and innovation. More importantly, the adoption of these strategies was more often than not a serious effort to assess institutional effectiveness, to improve program performance, and to enhance instructional modalities and student outcomes (p. 3).

What is new about today's concerns, Simmons continues, "is the stepped-up pace to find more effective instruments and approaches to assess student learning. In that regard, we have all become more actively engaged in the search for better institutional effectiveness criteria and the most appropriate alternative for assessing both institutional and student outcomes" (pp. 3-4).

This concern for evaluative criteria is reflected in the growing number of colleges and college systems that build their institutional research programs around indicators of institutional effectiveness. The compilation of indicators takes the institutional research function beyond day-to-day compliance reporting and requires colleges to organize data from otherwise unrelated reports in ways that provide insights into college strengths and weaknesses. Institutional responses to state mandates for assessment of college effectiveness in Virginia provide an illustration. The student assessment plan at Tidewater Community College, for example, organizes data from a variety of institutional sources into a matrix that provides a comprehensive look at student success in developmental, general education, transfer, and occupational curricula. Through the matrix, described in Figure Five, the college has clearly defined the sources and types of indicators that will be used to assess student progress in each of these program areas (Roesler, 1988). Feedback loops, though not illustrated in the matrix, allow for institutional action based on review of strengths and weaknesses of each area. Through these feedback loops, the indicators within the matrix may be subject to change over time.

The identification of such indicators is a central task in the development of student tracking systems, linking them to institutional evaluation and improvement. Indeed, student tracking systems are structured around indicators of student progress collected at regular intervals as students move in, through, and out of college. Those individuals building these data bases, then, often begin by determining which student progress indicators are most appropriate for the college and most telling of its effectiveness. Accordingly, this section of the monograph examines the nature and appropriate use of indicators, reviewing prior attempts to identify student success and other indicators that can properly be applied to community colleges.

What Is an Indicator?

Indicators are not outcomes. Defined "as something that points out, gives an indication of, or expresses briefly or generally," an indicator should be interpreted as a guidepost or warning flag, not as a precise measure (Renkiewicz and others, 1988, p. 6). For example, indicators of student outcomes might include the degree attainment rates of entering student cohorts, the number of credit hours

FIGURE FIVE
Assessment Matrix
Tidewater Community College (Va.)

ASSESSMENT PROCESS	ACADEMIC PROGRAMS			
	Developmental Studies	General Education	University Parallel	Occupational Technical

ENTRY EVALUATION	English
	  Comparative
	  Guidance and
	  Placement, with
	  Locally Developed
	  Writing Samples
	Mathematics
	  Local or Standardized
	  Placement Exam
		Open Admission
		
		Developmental Courses, if Needed
		
		Course Prerequisites
			Open Admission
			
			Developmental Courses, if Needed
			
			Course Prerequisites
				Open Admission
				Specific Admission
				  Requirements -
				  Selected Programs
				Developmental Courses, if Necessary
				Course Prerequisites

MONITORING PROCEDURES	Continuous Alert System Testing Based on Course Objectives	Continuous Alert System Testing Based on Course Objectives	Continuous Alert System Testing Based on Course Objectives	Continuous Alert System or Faculty Advising Testing Based on Course Objectives Testing of Skill Proficiency

EXIT EVALUATION	English -
	  Writing Exit Exam
	  Reading: Nelson
	    Denny Reading Test
	
	Mathematics -
	  80% Average in the
	  Developmental Course
		Summative Evaluation - Externally Validated Exam	Completion of AA or AS Degree Requirements
			
			Successful Completion of Courses with a "C" or Better Grade
				Competency in Basic Technical Skills
				
				Completion of All General Education and Technical Courses

FOLLOW-UP	Tracking -
	  English 101
	  English 111
	
	  Math 181
	  Math 161
	  Math 111
		Graduate Survey
		
		Employer Survey
			Tracking of Students at Four-year Institutions
			
			Graduate Survey
				Credentialing or Licensing Exam, Where Applicable
				
				Employer Survey
				
				Graduate Survey

POPULATION	Placement Testing -
	  All Students who Wish
	  to Enroll in English or
	  Mathematics
	
	Tracking - Continuing Students
		Exit Exam - 15% of Graduating Class: 5% AA, 30% AS, and 65% AAS
		
		Graduate Survey - All Graduates
		Employer Survey - All Graduates
			Tracking AA and AS Graduates
			
			Graduate Survey - All AA and AS Graduates
				Credentialing and Licensing Exams - Specific Program Graduates
				Graduate Survey - All Graduates
				Employer Survey - All Graduates

SCHEDULE	Placement Testing - Each Session Tracking - Each Session	Exit Exam - Spring Session Graduate Survey - Fall Session Employer Survey - Spring Session	Tracking: Annual Report from Four-year Institutions Graduate Survey - Fall Session	Credentialing and Licensing Exams Within 3 Months of Graduation Exit Exam - Spring Graduate Survey - Fall Employer Survey - Spring

Source: Roesler, 1988, p. 3.

completed per term as a percent of the number of credit hours attempted, or the percent of former students who indicate on follow-up surveys that they are "satisfied" or "very satisfied" with their college experience. While these indicators, collected year after year, may point to trends that bear further investigation, they do not of themselves measure what happens to students or gauge college effectiveness in meeting students needs. As Ewell (1983) points out:

> The indicative quality of most student outcomes research is probably the aspect least well understood by its critics. . . . Most procedures for gathering data on student outcomes are indirect and will provide only partial information on a given outcome. Information gathered in this manner is ordinarily much more useful for the questions it raises than for the answers it provides (p. 62).

An example of the use of indicators comes from the Maryland State Board for Community Colleges, which publishes an annual state profile of Maryland's public two-year institutions. For each community college, the performance profile draws upon annual student follow-up surveys and other institutional research studies to provide year-by-year trend data on the following five indicators:

- Percent of vocational program graduates who find full-time employment in fields related to their program of study;

- Percent of students who meet their transfer goal (that is, the transfer rates of graduates who enrolled *with the intention of transferring*);

- Percent of these transfer students (those who have transferred to senior institutions in Maryland) who rate their preparation for transfer as "good" or "very good;"

- Percent of employers who rate the training received by graduates as "good" or "very good;" and

- Percent of nursing graduates who pass their licensure examination on the first try.

These trend data are reported in a series of well-documented tables with limitations carefully spelled out (see Table Three for an example). Indeed, the Maryland State Board, cognizant of the danger of misinterpretation, adheres to six published principles in compiling and reporting the profile:

1. The variables used in the performance profile should be consistent with the mission and goals of the Maryland community college system.

2. Maryland community colleges are committed to excellence in achieving the broad purposes of education, and they set high expectations for students in developing critical thinking, clear expression, and responsible citizenship. In an operational sense, quality is measured by student success, primarily in transfer achievement and occupational performance.

3. Assessment of college performance should be done in terms of multiple measures. Colleges are complex organizations with several overlapping goals, and no single variable should be thought of as a complete measure of success.

4. Data for each variable should be displayed as trends over time.

5. The primary bodies responsible for analyzing and acting on the performance profile are the local community college boards of trustees. Each board bears the primary responsibility for establishing the policy directions and evaluating the success of the college.

TABLE THREE

Performance Profile: Career Credit Students
Maryland Community Colleges

College	Full-time Employment in Field of Training (a)(b)(c)				Employers Rating Training of Graduates Very Good or Good (a)				First-time Pass Rate for State Nursing Licensing Examination				
	1980 %	1982 %	1984 %	1986 %	1980 %	1982 %	1984 %	1986 %	1982 %	1983 %	1984 %	1985 %	1986 %
Allegany (AL)	51	47	50	48	92	88	98	91	98	85	90	91	92
Anne Arundel (AN)	67	62	61	56	78	96	96	94	97	94	97	97	97
Baltimore (BA)	51	44	51	46	95	88	84	81	98	93	94	95	100
Catonsville (CA)	59	62	70	63	90	93	87	91	96	95	95	92	90
Cecil (CE)	58	57	62	66	-	-	93	91	-	80	86	82	81
Charles (CHA)	62	57	63	57	93	94	89	96	92	87	88	83	84
Chesapeake (CHE)	-	60	60	63	-	-	93	96	-	-	-	-	-
Dundalk (DU)	44	42	56	45	92	75	96	92	-	-	-	-	-
Essex (ES)	59	59	64	63	88	84	85	86	94	91	92	93	92
Frederick (FR)	68	60	61	42	61	75	100	92	100	96	100	100	100
Garrett (GA)	40	39	42	50	-	-	-	-	-	-	-	-	-
Hagerstown (HG)	62	59	58	55	86	86	97	86	89	89	96	92	92
Harford (HR)	52	53	53	52	87	84	85	89	88	96	86	93	95
Howard (HO)	60	54	63	65	88	81	78	88	92	86	85	91	89
Montgomery (MO)	50	42	49	47	84	91	91	87	98	97	95	94	94
Prince George's (PR)	60	55	60	60	89	95	81	95	79	83	90	86	85
Wor-Wic Tech (WO)	50	48	64	56	-	94	90	90	100	92	97	100	100
Systemwide	56	53	58	55	87	89	89	90	93	90	92	95	92

- The purposes of the Performance Profile are to provide information to the colleges for self-improvement and to demonstrate institutional accountability.
- Each criterion should be viewed in relation to the trend over time at the college, similar colleges, and the financial resources at the college.
- A "-" (dash) designates total cell size smaller than 10 or data not available.

Footnotes:
(a) Graduates and employers were surveyed one year after graduation. In systemwide results, a variation of ± 2 percent could be due to sampling error. For the college results, variations of ± 5 percent could be due to sampling error.
(b) Includes AA certificate graduates who reported field of training directly or somewhat related to employment.
(c) Employment in field of training also varies by program and program area with higher rates in Health Services Technologies (60 percent) and Mechanical and Engineering Technologies (64 percent); and lower placement rates in Public Service Technologies (38 percent); Data Processing Technologies (51 percent), and Business and Commerce Technologies (56 percent).

Source: Maryland State Board for Community Colleges, 1988, p. 2.

6. The performance profile should be accompanied by an explanation of its purposes, methodology, and limitations (Maryland State Board for Community Colleges, 1988, p. 1).

Central to the principles underlying the compilation of the performance profile is the identification and prioritization—in an operational sense—of those outcomes that the state feels are the most important measures of institutional quality. In the case of Maryland, those priorities focus on student success, primarily in transfer achievement and occupational performance (see principle "2" above). The indicators used in the performance profile were determined accordingly. Given the multiple missions of the community college and the numerous fiscal, administrative, and educational effectiveness measures that could be used, each college or college system needs to engage in a decision-making process yielding a manageable set of indicators that can be the focus of institutional research in general and student tracking systems in particular. Moore (1986) maintains that this is a matter of building consensus:

> Because effectiveness is multidimensional and educational outcomes are multiple and diverse, it must be obvious that there can be no single criterion for institutional effectiveness. Rather, the challenge is to achieve consensus regarding appropriate clusters of criteria that are specific and observable and that also make sense to faculty members, administrators, students, policy makers, and the general public.

What Indicators Have Been Proposed for Community Colleges?

The literature cites many attempts to identify indicators of institutional effectiveness. Most of these attempts have resulted in relatively large catalogs of suggested indicators that are more complex than the five-part Maryland performance profile. In the struggle to balance the competing demands of cost-effectiveness on the one hand with completeness of coverage on the other, institutional leaders appear to lean toward the latter at the expense of the former. Examples are cited below.

AACJC Conference on Community College Research

As one of the most visible agencies representing the nation's community, technical, and junior colleges, the American Association of Community and Junior Colleges (AACJC) has long served as an information resource for community college policy makers. In an effort to improve the data available for policy makers, especially in the wake of demands for indicators of institutional effectiveness as it relates to student outcomes, AACJC convened a panel of community college presidents and researchers to specify the most pressing information needs. The meeting, held in fall 1987 and sponsored jointly by AACJC and the U.S. Department of Education's Office of Educational Research and Improvement, embraced three themes:

- Accountability--reporting information to external constituencies such as parents, legislators, alumni, employers, and the general public;

- Planning--providing an information base for management decision making; and

- Improvement--using information as the basis for faculty development, curriculum change, and the development of student support services.

The most pressing information need, the panel concluded, was for data on student flow and outcomes. Over the course of the meeting, participants recommended that college data collection and research focus on indicators of (1) student attributes, including student skill levels and educational objectives, (2) term-by-term student academic progress toward his or her goals, and (3) outcomes at the end of and following the student's tenure with the college. These indicators, outlined in Figure Six , are familiar items in student surveys and follow-up studies. The challenge posed by the panel, however, was whether AACJC or any other national agency could incorporate such measures in national data collection efforts, "assuring that information on student attributes is collected accurately according to consistent definitions and then related to student progress and outcomes" (Palmer, 1988, p. 43).

AACJC continues to work on the development of national student success indicators, though substantial progress in this area depends on the ability and willingness of individual colleges to collect data on the educational objectives of entering students in a consistent manner and then to tie these data on student goals to outcome indicators collected in longitudinal analyses of student flow and progress. Much will also depend on the ability of colleges to operationally define the indicators proposed by the conference participants. For example, the participants felt it important that student progress and outcomes be judged in light of the student's academic ability (measured at college entry). Limiting themselves to general guidelines, the conference participants left the details of how academic ability should be measured to individual colleges.

League for Innovation in the Community College

In another national effort aimed at developing guidelines for "Assessing Institutional Effectiveness in the Community College," the League for Innovation in the Community College is considering numerous outcomes indicators for each of five community college missions: transfer education; career/ preparation; continuing education; basic skills education; and the "access mission" (i.e., keeping the door of higher education open). After careful consideration of the clients, programs, and audiences associated with each of these missions, the statement, currently under development, will include indicators in the form of questions and suggested data sources. For example, under the transfer mission, the statement may recommend that the following questions, among others, be used to guide judgment of effectiveness:

Questions	Data Sources
What percentage of students who state transfer as their goal actually transfer?	Transcripts, enrollment profiles, student surveys
To what extent do students who transfer successfully complete their baccalaureate degrees? By major?	Four-year institution records; follow-up surveys of transfer students

As of this writing, the guidelines are still in draft form; the example above is used to illustrate the general format only. When the document is issued, however, it will be a signal reference tool, recommending numerous indicators and providing guidance for their use and interpretation. In addition, the statement should provide an excellent framework for practitioners deciding on indicators for their own institutions by stressing the importance of tying indicators to the college mission and using the results to inform institutional improvement. As the preliminary draft of the statement carefully explains, measures selected as indicators must be practical and relevant to the college mission, have a reasonable chance of improving institutional effectiveness, and be used in such a way that they do not rank-order or otherwise punish some programs at the expense of others (League for Innovation in the Community College, 1989).

FIGURE SIX

Indicators of Student Attributes, Progress, and Success, Suggested by Panel Members at the AACJC Conference on Community College Research, October 1987

I. <u>Attributes of Entering Students</u>

A. Immediate Student Educational Objective (Student to Indicate One):

1. Preparation for Transfer
2. Preparation for a New Job
3. Skills Upgrading for a Current Job
4. Personal Interest

B. Student Plans to Earn a Degree <u>at the Community College</u>

C. Highest Educational Credential Previously Earned

D. Time Elapsed Since Earning Last Credential

E. Indicators of Academic Ability at Entrance

II. <u>Student Progress Through the Institution</u>

A. Retention in Terms of Course Completion Rates and the Ratio of Credit Hours Completed to Credit Hours Attempted.

B. Academic Progress in Terms of the Change in a Student's Grade Point Average Over Time.

C. "Intensity" of Persistence as Measured by the Length of Time it Takes for Students to Achieve Their Goals.

III. <u>Student Outcomes After Graduating or Leaving the College</u>

A. Percent of Entering Students who Achieve Their Goals Within Five Years.

B. Performance of Graduates on Criterion-based Assessments Measuring Student Mastery of Higher-order Thinking Skills, Basic Computational and Verbal Skills, Major Subject Areas, and Perspectives Gained Through General Education.

C. Comparative Grade Point Averages of Transfer and Native Students at Four-year Colleges.

D. Bachelor's Degree Attainment of Community College Transfers.

E. Job Placement Rate of Vocational Graduates.

Source: Palmer, 1988.

California Association of Community Colleges

The California Association of Community Colleges (CACC) involved students, trustees, faculty members, and administrators in a study designed to (1) identify and rank-order appropriate indicators of institutional success; and (2) identify appropriate measures for each indicator. The study, conducted largely at the 1987 CACC Convention and at the April 1988 CACC Research Conference, resulted in a listing of 10 "top" indicators along with accompanying measures (See Figure Seven). Interestingly, the study participants gave higher priority rankings to process measures such as "positive faculty/student relationships," than to student outcomes measures, such as "retention of students," that are normally used in student tracking systems. This surprised the research directors, who hypothesize that practitioners may shy away from student outcomes because they are difficult to measure at the community college. As Renkiewicz and others (1989) explain,

> The initial list of indicators included both process and outcome indicators. The researchers were somewhat surprised when certain outcome indicators failed to be selected in the top 10 indicators. One reason for this may be that the professionals in the field realize that the procedures used to measure these outcomes can be very complex. Community college personnel may be concerned that a simplistic approach would provide distorted information which may be harmful to the college. For example, the issue of community college completers is a complex one. Who is a completer? A student who receives a degree or certificate? A student who learns a skill and takes a job? A student who earns enough units to transfer? As a follow-up, it would be beneficial to ask some representatives from the conference to indicate their perceptions about why these indicators were chosen as the most important (p. 7).

Community College of Philadelphia

At the Community College of Philadelphia (CCP), Pennsylvania, an ad hoc committee was appointed by the president in 1985 to design a program of comprehensive institutional evaluations. One of the first steps taken by the committee was to identify the varying ways in which effectiveness can be judged and choose those that should serve as the focus for the evaluation effort. Five areas of potential investigation were identified: (1) financial effectiveness; (2) enrollment effectiveness (as in the ability to achieve enrollment targets); (3) community impact (such as economic impact on the community or the extent to which the college meets area labor force needs); (4) educational effectiveness from an institutional perspective (as in the extent to which students master course competencies and program requirements); and (5) educational effectiveness from the student perspective, as in the extent to which the students' educational and personal goals are met. The committee decided to focus on the latter two, emphasizing that institutional evaluation should be guided by *educational* indicators (as opposed to administrative or fiscal ones), that these indicators should stress both cognitive and non-cognitive outcomes, and that "a significant effort would be placed on understanding students' educational goals at the time they first enrolled, and in understanding how they changed while they were at the college" (Hawk, 1987, p. 4).

As part of the evaluation effort, CCP developed a set of performance indicators to be compiled annually for all programs and used to assess trends in student enrollment and success. The indicators, outlined in Figure Eight, may be computed for race, sex, and age, showing how students with differing characteristics fare in terms of retention, academic performance, subsequent employment, or subsequent education. Collection of data for these indicators is only one part of a larger research effort that includes classroom-based research focusing on teacher effectiveness and institutional research on topics of special interest, such as analyses of the factors that contribute to retention or the impact graduates have on the surrounding labor market. Thus, the indicators are used to guide further, in-depth studies and are

FIGURE SEVEN

Measures for Top 10 Indicators (CACC Study)

1. — Faculty Effectiveness
    A. Retention rates from 1st census to 2nd census to end of term.
    B. Degree to which students meet stated course objectives.
    C. Student perceptions of faculty effectiveness.

2. — Student Satisfaction with Quality of Instruction
    A. Currently enrolled students' perceptions of instructors from required, standardized evaluation form.
    B. Students' self-reports upon exiting a course.
    C. Students' self-reports gathered after leaving (within a time interval, e.g.: one semester later).

3. — Positive Faculty/Student Relationships
    A. Students' perceptions of faculty as positive role models.
    B. Did student feel recognized as an individual in this class?
    C. Does instructor give adequate feedback regarding student progress?

4. — Financial Viability*
    A. Proportion of expenditures used from reserves for college operation.
    B. Percent of general reserves to annual budget.
    C. Expenditures per unit of workload.
    D. Extent of financial planning.

5. — Effectiveness of Administrative Staff
    A. Ability to motivate college community.
    B. Staff morale.
    C. Evidence of key decisions being linked to planning process.
    D. The extent faculty/staff are involved in decision-making process.

6. — Student Satisfaction with Services (What a College Provides Outside Classroom)
    A. Satisfaction survey while in attendance (a student at the college).
    B. Satisfaction survey after leaving (after separation from college).
    C. Satisfaction survey at time of service delivery.
    D. Student interviews assessing their experience.

7. — Positive Reaction of Staff to Students
    A. Perceptions of students assessing helpfulness of college staff.
    B. Staff satisfaction with job environment.
    C. Frequency with which students make use of faculty office hours.
    D. Instructors' attitudes of student learning.

8. — Community Perception of the College
    A. Solicited community attitudes using various methods (written surveys, telephone contacts, focused interviews) of various groups such as employers, high school counselors, under-represented populations. Formal needs assessment including perceived attitudes is the most comprehensive method.
    B. Percent of local high school graduates attending college.
    C. Participation rate of population of the District in college activities.
    D. Number of requests for service from business, industry, and other agencies.

9. — Adequate Facilities to Support College Programs
    A. Number of hours of room availability compared to number of hours used.
    B. Flexibility, adaptability of floor space to meet changing needs.
    C. Adequacy of equipment to meet current instructional needs.

10. — Retention of Students
    A. Total units completed, divided by total units attempted at 1st census (unit earned rate).
    B. Re-enrollment rates (over time).

Source: Renkiewicz and others, 1988, pp. 5-6.
* All measures should be assessed over time (5 years).

FIGURE EIGHT

Proposed Program Performance Indicators
Community College of Philadelphia

A. Enrollment Patterns

FTE enrollment - all students by term, annual
FTE enrollment - new students by term, annual
Headcount - new students enrolled
Headcount - full-time students
Total petitioners by term and year
Total new student applications received by term and year
% of new student applications received that enrolled by term and year
New student and petitioner headcount as % of new student enrollment goal
Headcount - petitioners enrolled by term and year
FTE - petitioners enrolled by term and year
% of headcount - new students entering at remedial, underprepared, and college-ready levels
% of students having sophomore status

B. Retention Patterns

Number of graduates by year
Number of graduates relative to students new to program per year
Number of returning students divided by new students per term and by year
Number of students who left with under 30 credits as a % of mean number of new and petition students - prior three years
Number of graduates as a % of mean number of new and petitioning students in prior three years
% of total headcount not graduating who returned next term (excluding summer)
% of headcount who have completed 24+ credits

C. Academic Performance Patterns

Median GPA - all students
Median GPA - full-time students
Median GPA - sophomore students
Median GPA - freshmen students
Number dropped for poor scholarship by term
Number dropped for poor progress by term
Number on academic probation due to poor scholarship
Number on academic probation due to poor progress
Mean value of credits earned divided by credits attempted
% of annual headcount enrollment dropped for academic standards reasons
% of annual headcount enrollment placed on probation for academic standards reasons
% of sophomore students having earned a passing grade in ENGL 102
% of graduates who were not initially degree-oriented
% of leavers who were initially degree-oriented

D. Post - CCP Outcomes

% graduates employed
% graduates employed in related field
% graduates transferring
% graduates unemployed and seeking work
% leavers employed
% leavers employed in related field
% leavers transferring
% leavers unemployed and seeking work
% leavers and graduates indicating educational goals were accomplished at the college
% indicating satisfaction with overall CCP experience

Source: Hawk, 1987, pp. 17-20.

not used by themselves to make judgments about program or institutional effectiveness. Hawk (1987) provides a complete description of the CCP institutional effectiveness program.

Florida Community College at Jacksonville

Institutional evaluation at Florida Community College at Jacksonville (FCCJ) is gauged, at least in part, by a set of performance indicators, each linked to six "strategic issues priorities": (1) assurance of high quality instruction; (2) hiring and retaining the right faculty and staff; (3) maintaining a viable mix of academic programs; (4) efficiency and effectiveness of management practices; (5) maintenance of a strong financial condition; and (6) assurance of a sound financial management. Thus, unlike the Community College of Philadelphia, which decided to focus on student-related outcomes, FCCJ has opted for a broader array of indicators, including both educational and administrative variables. An outline of the strategic performance indicators related to student flow and success is presented in Figure Nine.

A key element in the use of these indicators lies in their clear presentation. Data for each indicator are presented in a timeline trend format, providing for an examination of year-to-year changes. In addition, the indicator is precisely explained, leaving no doubt as to how it was calculated. The care taken in reporting indicators of institutional effectiveness reflects the college's sensitivity to the potential misuse of such data and mirrors the guidelines set by the state of Maryland for the performance profile of its community colleges. See Figure Ten for an example of how one indicator—percentage of students who pass the CLAST (College-Level Academic Skills Test) on the first try—is displayed by FCCJ as a trend over time.

FIGURE NINE	
Selected Strategic Performance Indicators of Student Success **Florida Community College at Jacksonville**	
Indicator	What Is Measured
CLAST scores (College-Level Academic Skills Test)	Percent of all first-time test takers who pass all four subtests
Follow-up findings, vocational completers	Percent who find job placements
Follow-up findings, AA degree recipients who transfer	Cumulative, upper-division grade point average of AA transfers in the state university system
GED (high school equivalency test)	Percent of FCCJ-prepared test takers who earn a GED, compared to the percent of all test takers who earn a GED
Grades	Grade distribution of enrolled students
Goal attainment	Percent of students who attain their goals
College preparatory remedial education	Percent of students assessed and enrolled into college preparatory courses who complete the course(s) with a "D" or better
Student satisfaction	Percent of student survey respondents who indicate that they are satisfied with the college's services and instruction
Source: Florida Community College at Jacksonville, 1989.	

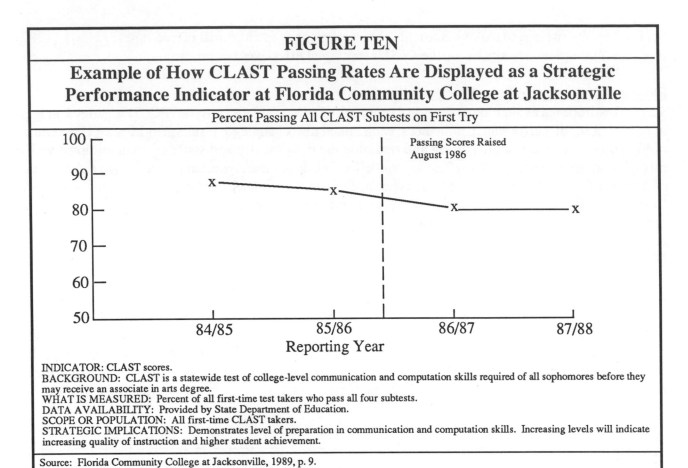

FIGURE TEN

Example of How CLAST Passing Rates Are Displayed as a Strategic Performance Indicator at Florida Community College at Jacksonville

Percent Passing All CLAST Subtests on First Try

INDICATOR: CLAST scores.
BACKGROUND: CLAST is a statewide test of college-level communication and computation skills required of all sophomores before they may receive an associate in arts degree.
WHAT IS MEASURED: Percent of all first-time test takers who pass all four subtests.
DATA AVAILABILITY: Provided by State Department of Education.
SCOPE OR POPULATION: All first-time CLAST takers.
STRATEGIC IMPLICATIONS: Demonstrates level of preparation in communication and computation skills. Increasing levels will indicate increasing quality of instruction and higher student achievement.

Source: Florida Community College at Jacksonville, 1989, p. 9.

Los Rios Community College District

Institutional research at the Los Rios Community College District (California) centers around a "student flow research model" that emphasizes data on students flowing through, into, and out of the college. Coffey (1987) points out that the model is built on seven key questions:

- What is our community like, and who are our potential students?

- Who are our enrolled students? Do they differ by college? Do they reflect the community at large?

- What kinds of preparation do our students bring to our institutions? Are they prepared for our college-level classes or do they need remediation?

- What are the educational goals of our students, and do these goals differ by age, sex, ethnicity, work status, or economic level?

- How well are we meeting our students' needs? Is what we're doing working, and how do we know?

- What happens to our students once they leave? Are they successful as transfers to four-year institutions? In finding jobs? In improving skills and earnings potential if currently employed?

- Finally, how can we improve what we're doing?

Coffey emphasizes the importance of beginning the institutional evaluation effort with research questions, and not simply with data that are readily available. Though the Los Rios Community College District, like most colleges, had quite a bit of data in various computer files, much of the data had to be reconfigured to meet the needs of the student flow model. As Coffey explains: "We decided early in the process to keep the <u>questions and answers</u> primary and the <u>data</u> secondary. In short, we didn't ask 'what can we do with all this data?' but 'what questions do we want to answer about our students, our programs, and our services?' " (Coffey, 1987, pp. 2-3).

Using the seven key questions as a foundation for student research districtwide, the student flow research model incorporates numerous studies, including special program evaluations and student surveys. One of the many products of this effort is a set of outcomes indicators tied to the students' educational objectives. Each year the district surveys graduates and non-returning students to assess their educational and occupational activities. In addition, the survey questionnaire asks about the students' educational objectives:

What was your PRIMARY objective in attending college (check one)?

_____ Improvement of existing "job skills"
_____ Preparation for job to be obtained
_____ University transfer credit
_____ Personal interest
_____ Other

Student responses to questions on their educational and occupational activities can be cross-tabulated against their educational goals to provide more meaningful outcomes indicators. For example, only 28 percent of all the respondents to the 1987 follow-up survey indicated that they had transferred to a four-year college or university. But this compared to 63.2 percent of the respondents who indicated that they enrolled *with the intention of preparing for transfer*. (Table Four details selected outcomes indicators calculated on the basis of follow-up surveys conducted in 1984, 1985, 1986, and 1987. For complete details, see Lee [1987]).

TABLE FOUR							
Indicators of Student Transfer and Employment Success, By Student Educational Objective Los Rios Community College District							
	Students who Enrolled with Intention of Transferring				Students who Enrolled to Prepare for a New Job			
	Year of Survey				Year of Survey			
% of Respondents who Are:	1984	1985	1986	1987	1984	1985	1986	1987
• Employed	59%	64%	66%	75%	79%	80%	85%	84%
• Not in labor force	32%	30%	28%	18%	10%	9%	7%	9%
• Unemployed, actively seeking	10%	6%	6%	7%	11%	10%	8%	7%
• Enrolled at a four-year college	71%	69%	69%	63%	12%	9%	8%	9%
• Re-enrolled at a community college	5%	9%	9%	8%	8%	18%	19%	17%
Source: Lee, 1987.								

This brief description does not do justice to the wide scope of research activities encompassed by the student flow research model. Indeed, follow-up surveys are only one of the model's many components. But it does show the potential of linking student outcomes to student intentions. As long as these intentions are assessed consistently over time (that is, as long as the same methodology and questions are used each year to assess intentions), researchers can calculate indicators of how well colleges help students meet their educational goals. The student follow-up component of the Los Rios student flow research model, like the Maryland performance profile discussed earlier, is an example of how that consistency works to the benefit of the research effort.

Miami-Dade Community College

Miami-Dade Community College's interest in indicators of institutional effectiveness has already been noted in the discussion of the college's effort to derive measures of student success that appropriately reflect the college mission without yielding self-serving results (see pages 21-22 of this monograph). In a recent report (Belcher, 1989), the college expands its base of indicators, drawing upon several institutional research studies to inform discussions of six areas of college effectiveness:

- The degree to which the college is successful in attracting area resident and high school graduates;

- The degree to which the college meets students' expectations;

- The degree to which the college meets the needs of the academically underprepared, non-native speakers of English, and academically talented students;

- The degree to which students successfully move through the system, meeting standards of academic progress;

- The degree to which associate degree graduates enroll in the upper division or secure job placements; and

- The degree to which students pass licensure or certification examinations.

These indicators, outlined in Figure Eleven, provide a mixed and thought-provoking picture when used in analyses of student success, indicating that while students who follow prescribed courses of study do well, many others may fall through the cracks. For example, Belcher (1989) found that persistence rates for students who successfully complete the prescribed college preparatory (remedial) program are as high as the persistence rates of those students who never need college preparatory assistance. Nonetheless, she also found that fewer than half of the students needing preparatory work complete the prescribed remedial coursework, even though they remain enrolled in the college (see Table Five). Many students, therefore, may remain at risk because they do not take advantage of college support services. As another example, the Miami-Dade data show that associate degree recipients do quite well after graduation; 65 to 70 percent of the associate in arts degree graduates enroll in the Florida State University or in the upper-division at local private colleges. Yet since the imposition of the CLAST requirement in 1984, the number of associate in arts graduates has declined, especially for minorities (see Table Six).

How should these data be interpreted? The Miami-Dade researchers cautiously note that indicators of institutional effectiveness are guides to further analysis and not definitive outcomes measures in themselves. "In essence, we have presented a competency checklist for our institution," Belcher (1989) explains. "We leave it to our readers to decide on a letter grade and where they would

FIGURE ELEVEN

Selected Indicators of Institutional Effectiveness
Miami-Dade Community College (MDCC)

Attracting Students to MDCC	Meeting Student Expectations	Meeting Students' Special Needs	Moving Students Successfully Through the Institution	Activities After the Associate Degree	Certifying Student Competencies
• % of Dade County high school graduates who enroll in MDCC • Proportion of adults in Dade County who enroll in MDCC • % of students who tested at MDCC, but who failed to subsequently enroll	• Degree to which students responding to a survey indicate that MDCC meets their expectations of the "ideal" college in the following areas: -faculty and staff -advising and counseling -general education -careers -institutional prestige and quality -financial aid -facilities -student orientation	• % of students in need of remedial work who complete prescribed courses • % of English-as-a-Second Language (ESL) students who complete prescribed ESL work • % of academically talented students who transfer to four-year colleges	• % of first-time students who return immediately for a subsequent, second semester • Passing grades awarded as a percent of all grades awarded • % of full-time degree seekers who, after three years, either graduated, left the college in good academic standing, or were still enrolled in good standing • Persistence and graduation rates of ESL students and of academically underprepared students • Associate degree recipients' graduation rates	• Transfer rates of A.A. graduates • Baccalaureate attainment rates of transfer • Job placement rates of A.S. graduates	• Passing rate of MDCC students on Florida's College-Level Academic Skills Test (CLAST) • Passing rates of MDCC students on licensure examinations, compared with statewide pass rates

Source: Belcher, 1989.

TABLE FIVE

Three-Year Persistence Rates (Graduated or Re-enrolled) for Tested First-Time-in-College Students Who Entered Miami-Dade Community College in Fall Term 1982 Based on Completion of College Preparatory Work

Students who Scored Below Placement Cut-off Score in:	Total Group							
	Successfully Completed College Preparatory Work in:							
	No Area		One Area		Two Areas		Three Areas	
	No.	%	No.	%	No.	%	No.	%
No Areas (N=2,021)								
N=	2,021							
Graduated	533	26						
Still Enrolled	430	21						
Total	963	47						
One Area (N=1,524)								
N=	873		651					
Graduated	95	11	136	21				
Still Enrolled	149	17	164	25				
Total	244	28	300	46				
Two Areas (N=1,360)								
N=	530		509		321			
Graduated	25	5	56	11	49	15		
Still Enrolled	47	9	130	26	104	33		
Total	72	14	186	37	153	48		
Three Areas (N=1,457)								
N=	641		357		303		156	
Graduated	7	1	12	4	24	8	14	9
Still Enrolled	56	19	69	19	89	29	58	37
Total	63	10	81	23	113	47	72	46

Source: Belcher, 1989, p.32.

TABLE SIX

Declines in the Number of Associate of Arts Graduates at Miami-Dade Community College Since the Implementation of CLAST (College-Level Academic Skills Test)

Ethnic Category	No. of A.A. Graduates 1983-84, Before CLAST Standards	No. of A.A. Graduates, 1987-88	Percent Change 1983 to 1987	1987-88 CLAST Examinees who Passed Fewer than Four Subtests*
White Non-Hispanic	1,339	967	-27.8%	128
Black Non-Hispanic	499	258	-48.3%	193
Hispanic	2,224	1,426	-35.9%	481
Total, All Ethnic	4,171	2,707	-35.1%	841

*All September 1987 A.A. examinees and all March and June 1988 first-time A.A. examinees who self-declared that they were ready to graduate.

Source: Belcher, 1989, p. 33.

comment that Miami-Dade 'needs improvement' or 'has accomplished the job very well' " (p. 14). Like the Los Rios Community College District, Miami-Dade has organized its institutional research data in such a way that it addresses, in a neutral format, clearly defined questions of college effectiveness in promoting student success.

Prince George's Community College

Prince George's Community College (PGCC) has issued a *Student Outcomes Performance Accountability Report* (Clagett, 1988), that charts trends in eight areas:

- Student course pass rates (percentage of those who receive a passing grade—as opposed to failure or withdrawal);

- Student retention (fall to spring retention rate, as well as the eight-year attendance/ retention pattern of students entering the college in 1980);

- Transfer, as measured by the fall-to-fall movement of PGCC students to Maryland four-year colleges and universities;

- Transfer, as measured by the percentage of graduates who indicate on follow-up surveys that they are attending a four-year college or university and by responses to questions concerning their academic progress and satisfaction with their preparation at the community college;

- The employment experiences of occupational program graduates as measured by follow-up surveys;

- Employer evaluations of graduates' job performance;

- Pass rates of graduates on licensure examinations;

- General education outcomes, as well as student self-assessments of the degree to which PGCC helped them in 11 general education areas (see Figure Twelve).

Many of the indicators in PGCC's accountability report are part of the Maryland performance profile discussed earlier. But others are unique to the college. The general education indicator, for example, was included after a college task force on institutional assessment determined that the college's assessment activities, while strong on most points, were weak in determining the students' growth in general education and higher-level cognitive skills. Rather than adding a testing component to the college's assessment effort, it was decided (at least for the time being) to amend the college's graduate survey so that it collected self-assessments of general education competency.

FIGURE TWELVE

Graduates' Responses to General Education Question Survey
Prince George's Community College

To what Extent Did Your Attendance at PGCC Help You Accomplish the Following?

	A Great Deal		A Fair Amount		Not at All
	5	4	3	2	1
Improve your reading comprehension	17%	32%	31%	10%	10%
Improve your writing	20	31	34	7	8
Increase your ability to use mathematics	16	31	30	12	11
Improve your ability to understand the logic and merits of arguments	19	30	31	10	9
Improve your understanding of science and technology	21	28	31	8	12
Increase your attentiveness to news and world events	17	26	31	12	13
Increase your knowledge of other cultures and periods of history	12	22	32	16	18
Expand or enhance your appreciation of art, music, or literature	14	18	24	12	31
Clarify your educational or career goals	35	32	22	6	5
Enhance your self-confidence	37	33	22	5	3
Increase your enjoyment of learning	43	32	18	4	3

Source: Clagett, 1988, p. 63.

Summary

Numerous indicators have been selected or proposed by community college researchers to help gauge institutional effectiveness, and as the examples presented here show, many of these indicators focus on retention and other student outcomes rather than on the administrative or quantitive measures that have traditionally guided the accreditation process. Some of these indicators can be derived from student records, graduate follow-up surveys, test scores, and other data sources that are usually available to institutional researchers. Examples cited in the literature include, among others, the following:

- Student course and credit-hour completion rates per term in both remedial and college-level classes;

- Changes in student grade point average from one term to another;

- Term retention rates (that is, the retention of students from the first census date, to the second census date, to the end of the term);

- Between-term retention rates, often calculated as the percent of first-time students who re-enroll for a second term;

- The number of graduates each year (sometimes displayed as a percentage of the number of students entering each year);

- The number of students dropped each term for academic reasons (where standards of academic performance are enforced);

- Percent of full-time, degree-seeking students who, after three years, have either graduated, left the college in good academic standing, or remained enrolled in good academic standing;

- Percent of vocational program graduates employed full-time in fields related to their programs of study at the community college;

- Self-reported transfer rates of those follow-up respondents who indicate that they originally enrolled at the community college with the intention of preparing for transfer to a four-year college or university;

- Percent of follow-up survey respondents who indicate that they were satisfied with their experience at the community college or who indicate that they met the goals that they set for themselves when they originally enrolled;

- Percent of graduates passing licensure examinations (where required);

- Percent of students satisfied each term with their classes (as determined by end-of-term student evaluations of classes and faculty);

- Percent of students passing "rising junior" examinations (such as Florida's College-Level Academic Skills Test);

- General education outcomes as determined by student pass rates selected in terms of their appropriateness to both the institution's curriculum and students;

- General education outcomes as determined by students' self-ratings of the degree to which the college has improved their knowledge and ability in the arts and sciences.

Other indicators, particulary those related to longer-term transfer outcomes, can only be calculated with data over which the community college has no control and which are therefore more difficult to come by. Such indicators include the baccalaureate attainment rates of former community college students and the degree to which the upper-division grade point averages of these students compare with the grade point averages of native university students.

Properly used, indicators of student outcomes can arouse curiosity about institutional effectiveness, pointing to areas that might warrant investigation. For example, the student self-assessments of general education skills detailed earlier in Figure Twelve might lead faculty at Prince George's Community College to examine ways of increasing students' exposure to the fine and performing arts; of all the general education areas listed, PGCC students were more likely to point to this area as one in which their skills and appreciation had not increased while enrolled in college. Selecting the most appropriate indicators for the college, then, is an important part of the college's evaluation effort. By helping in this selection process, collecting the requisite data, and reporting the indicators in an informative, thought-provoking manner, institutional researchers become key players in college planning and improvement, not just data managers who fulfill reporting requirements. As the examples highlighted in this section of the monograph illustrate, the successful use of indicators depends on a number of factors:

- Selecting indicators that are directly tied to the college mission, that can be operationally defined, and that have a reasonable chance of pointing to areas that are key to institutional improvement;

- Making sure that indicators are selected in response to questions that need answering and not simply on the basis of available data;

- Involving different college constituencies in selecting the indicators, as was the case in the indicators' research project conducted by the California Association of Community Colleges, and making sure that constituencies understand their purpose;

- Reporting indicators in such a way that they are used to foster improvement, rather than rank-order or otherwise "punish" some programs at the expense of others;

- Recognizing the limitations of indicators as pointers or flags, and advising against their misuse as absolute outcomes measures;

- Compiling reports that carefully explain the methodology used in calculating the indicators and display the indicators as trend data showing changes over time.

To date, however, community college experience with such indicators appears to be quite limited, and many discussions of indicators present wish lists, suggesting information gaps that need to be filled. Examples of these wish lists include the catalog of indicators suggested by participants of AACJC's 1988 Conference on Community College Research (Palmer, 1988) and by the California Association of Community Colleges (Renkiewicz and others, 1988). In neither case have these indicators been routinely operationalized at the community college. Where indicator programs are in place, they are most often based on cross-sectional rather than longitudinal data. For example, some indicators of student goal attainment based on follow-up surveys of former students ask (1) what was your goal upon college entrance? and (2) did you meet it? This one-shot method, while providing valuable insights into the degree to which former students feel they've met their goals, does not yield a picture of how a student's goals change from semester to semester or how students with different goals progress through the community college. More robust indicators of student flow await longitudinal analyses. The next section reviews the literature dealing with the construction of tracking systems for community colleges and the indicators that form the basis of those systems.

PART FOUR:

INCORPORATING INDICATORS INTO STUDENT TRACKING SYSTEMS

INCORPORATING INDICATORS INTO
STUDENT TRACKING SYSTEMS

Student tracking systems are part of the response to demands that institutional accountability be grounded on the assessment of student progress and outcomes. As longitudinal data bases built around indicators that document the educational progress of student cohorts on a term-by-term basis, tracking systems change the focus of institutional research from such questions as "How many students are enrolled?" or "What is the current expenditure per student?" to more telling questions such as "Which of our students meet their educational goals?" or "Do remedial programs successfully prepare students for college-level work?" Going beyond simple indicators used by some community colleges to gauge outcomes, tracking systems help trace the paths students take toward those outcomes, detailing how those paths may vary for students with differing backgrounds, abilities, and educational attainments.

The basic design of student tracking systems is easily understood. A cohort of entering students is identified, and a longitudinal data base is built that includes (1) data on the students' goals and on selected attributes that students bring with them to the college; (2) indicators of the term-by-term enrollment and academic progress of the cohort; and (3) indicators of student outcomes after the students leave the college. The data base allows for an analysis of student flow through the institution and for cross-tabulations of student attributes with outcomes indicators. For example, a tracking system would enable a college to determine the percentage of entering students who earn the associate degree within four years. This completion rate can be cross-tabulated against the students' initial degree goals in order to calculate a more telling indicator of degree completion: the graduation rate of those students who enroll with the intention of earning an associate degree. This indicator, in turn, can be examined along any number of attributes, including age, race, or academic ability.

In developing these data bases, a series of decisions, discussed at length by Ewell (1987b), must be made:

- *Who will be tracked?* All students? Credit students who have initiated a matriculation process? Credit students who have completed a minimum number of courses? Because of the large number of community college students who enroll for one course in one term, the size of the tracking system can be reduced significantly by including only students who have matriculated (if such a process is in place) or who otherwise demonstrate a potential for systematic study. In brief, the college must decide if it will track all students or only those who can be categorized as matriculated students.

- *How long — or over how many terms — should the students be tracked?* Much depends on the mortality rate of the student cohort. Ewell (1987b) suggests that "a good rule of thumb. . .is to maintain a tracking period of sufficient length to determine the fates of at least 90 percent of the students in the cohort" (p.10). Much will depend on what we want to know about students. Tracking outcomes after students leave the college will require a longer period of operation than tracking persistence and attainment while the students are enrolled in the college.

- *How often will new cohorts be tracked?* Ewell points out that while it may be possible to begin a new tracking cohort each term, it may not be practical or necessary. "There is. . .relatively little variation in results across cohorts from successive years. . . . As a result, most institutions establish new cohorts on a periodic basis--for example, once every three years. A more complicated issue is whether to establish cohorts for terms other than fall" (p.10).

- *What data elements will be tracked each term?* The answer to this question will likely be a compromise between what researchers would like to know and what data are available. For example, the college might want to compare the outcomes of students with deferring socioeconomic (SES) backgrounds. But finding proxy measure for SES is difficult, and the college may decide to forgo this analysis and concentrate on others for which data are available.

A final question, discussed by Ewell, Parker, and Jones (1988), focuses on data processing: How will data from various college offices be merged into a single cohort tracking file? Colleges may find that much of the data they need are dispersed throughout the campus in computers that may not be compatible and in file formats that may not be consistent. For example, student placement scores (used as indicators of academic ability) may be filed in a counseling office, while grades and indicators of student educational goals may be on record at the registrar's office. A major challenge then is to find ways of pulling all of these data together.

Student Tracking Systems

The following paragraphs draw upon the literature and other sources to review student tracking models and discuss problems faced by colleges in the construction of these longitudinal data bases. Because community colleges have had, as of this writing, only limited experience in operating student tracking systems, much of the literature is theoretical, focusing more on the purpose and designs of tracking systems than on the more practical problems of operation and use.

Eastern New Mexico State University

Wilkinson (1985) proposed a student tracking system designed to track every third freshman class at Eastern New Mexico State University (ENMSU) from the time of arrival until about three years after leaving the university. While Wilkinson does not outline the indicators used in the tracking system, he does describe the process used to plan for the system's initiation. Central to this process is a three-part division of labor, involving:

- A steering/advisory committee designed to assure broad campus participation and to "ensure that the data collected is of use for 'educational' improvement and policymaking" (Wilkinson, 1985, p. 6);

- Institutional research personnel, who provide direct staff support to the advisory committee;

- The registrar and/or chief admissions officer who would be charged with the data collection task and other day-to-day operations.

Interestingly, the advisory committee has a broad charge and was involved in specifying the underlying research questions, as well as detailing the construction of the data base. As Wilkinson (1985) explains:

The role of the committee will be: (1) to develop the specific research questions that will guide this study and dictate the type of data to be collected; (2) to provide guidance to the study and provide insight to possible improvements in design and data analysis; (3) to develop specific guidelines for the implementation and continual operation of the study; (4) to oversee the continual evaluation of the study. . . ; and (5) authorizing data analysis and distribution of reports. . . . The committee is an integral component to the success of this study with its importance far exceeding the initial design and implementation of data collection. It is the charge of the committee to keep the study current and "timely" as well as to generate and distribute reports (p. 6).

Figure Thirteen details the structure of ENMSU's proposed student tracking system, which utilizes a number of surveys to gather information from students at several points: at entrance; upon withdrawal or dropping out; upon attainment of sophomore status; at graduation; and later on as alumni. While appropriate for a four-year institution, ENMSU's system may be too simple for community colleges. The stop-in, stop-out pattern of community college attendance will require term-by-term assessments of student flow. Nonetheless, the three-part cooperation of an advisory committee, the registrar's office, and the institutional research office seems a promising approach for any institution.

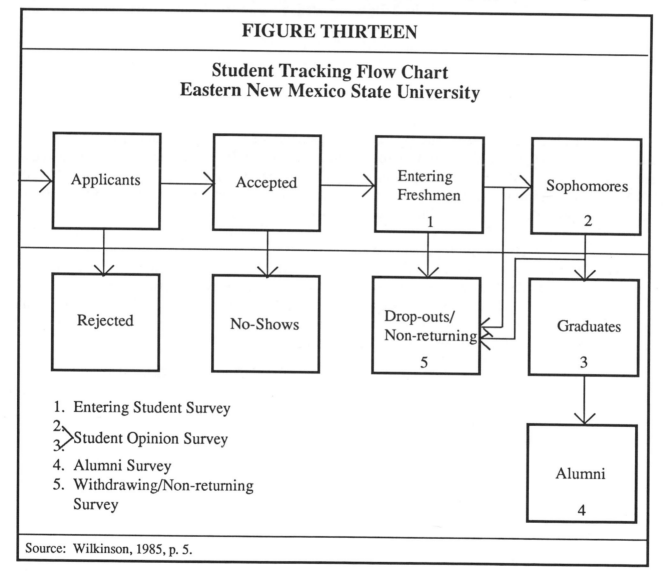

FIGURE THIRTEEN

Student Tracking Flow Chart
Eastern New Mexico State University

1. Entering Student Survey
2. Student Opinion Survey
3.
4. Alumni Survey
5. Withdrawing/Non-returning Survey

Source: Wilkinson, 1985, p. 5.

Arapahoe Community College

Researchers at Arapahoe Community College (Colorado) have proposed a simplified longitudinal model that is designed to track entering student cohorts over an eight-term period. The model, detailed by Voorhees and Hart (1989), relates student outcomes to two attributes: (1) academic ability as determined by test scores; and (2) student goals, which are updated each term in an effort to "articulate institutional outcomes from a student perspective" (p. 35). Another feature of the model is its compactness. The term-by-term indicators of student progress are limited to the ratio of hours attempted to hours completed, the student's cumulative grade point average, and a flag indicating whether or not the student's goal has been attained. In an effort to keep the file manageable, other indicators (such as course enrollment or course grades) are omitted.

Nonetheless, Voorhees and Hart indicate that the model poses a challenging task: " . . . not all institutions collect the breadth of information suggested here, and this information may be impossible to obtain for past terms" (p. 34). A further difficulty is the need to merge multiple term files, a task that requires practiced knowledge of data base software packages. Size is another problem. In maintaining the data base, Voorhees and Hart recommend that the number of variables included in the data base be kept to a minimum and that the longitudinal file be updated twice a term: "once at the institution's census date to collect current information on work status, economic disability, and student goal status, and again at the end of the term to collect hours completed and GPA" (p. 36). Even when following the simplified model proposed by Voorhees and Hart, each student record includes 108 bits of information when carried over a period of eight terms.

LONESTAR Student Tracking System

The LONESTAR student tracking system, developed for the Texas community colleges by the National Center for Higher Education Management Systems (NCHEMS), is the most widely known system in use today. More detailed than the Arapahoe model discussed by Voorhees and Hart, the LONESTAR (Longitudinal Student Tracking and Reporting) system was designed to meet several objectives: to provide management information for institutional improvement; to provide a framework for the uniform reporting of institutional effectiveness data to the Texas Coordinating Board of Higher Education; and to "evaluate and report on the effectiveness of the remediation function of community colleges as a primary access point to higher education in the state" (Ewell, Parker, and Jones, 1988, p. 2). Because the LONESTAR system was developed for uniform use by all Texas community colleges (with their different data collection and processing systems), NCHEMS staff recognized that they would need to do more than specify a model in only general terms. As the NCHEMS researchers explain, "implementing LONESTAR involved the development of :

- a common methodology for identifying the types of students to be included in the system;

- common procedures for determining how individual tracking records were to be constructed, handled, and maintained;

- a list of commonly defined data elements that all institutions were to include in the system;

- a set of optional data elements that institutions might include at their discretion;

- a set of recommended reports for local institutional use and for submitting information to the Coordinating Board; and

- a set of recommended procedures for installing and operating the system locally using hardware and software" (Ewell, Parker, and Jones, 1988, pp. 2-3).

As a result, the document describing the LONESTAR system — *Establishing a Longitudinal Student Tracking System: An Implementation Handbook* (Ewell, Parker, and Jones, 1988)— is the most comprehensive technical resource available on longitudinal student tracking at community colleges, detailing both recommended data elements and outlining methodologies for constructing the data base itself. The data elements summarized in Figure Fourteen and detailed in Appendix One allow researchers

FIGURE FOURTEEN

Selected LONESTAR Data Elements

Attributes	Term-by-Term Indicators	Follow-Up Indicators for Graduates/Leavers (All Optional)

Student Identification No.
Demographics
    gender
    date of birth
    ethnicity
    citizenship
Residence(in-state, out-of-state, etc.)
Physical Disability/Learning Disability
Economic or Academic Disadvantagement
Current Employment Status
Educational Background
    last high school attended
    type of high school certificate
      awarded
    date of high school graduation
    high school grade point average
    last college attended
    previous college-level academic
      experience
Remediation Status at Time of Entry
    reading
    writing
    computation
    English proficiency
Enrollment Status
    first term of academic history
    admission status (full, provisional)
    basis of admission (high school
    graduate, individual approval, etc.)
Financial Aid Status
Time of Attendance (day, evening, etc.)
Location of Instruction (on-campus,
  off-campus)
Initial Program at Time of Entry
Program Track (vocational, academic,
  unclassified)
Student Objective (primary reason for
  enrolling)
Intended Duration (one term only,
  two terms, etc.)
Term of Enrollment in First College-
  Level English Class
Performance in First College-Level
  English Class
Term of Enrollment in First College-
  Level Math Class
Performance in First College-Level
  Math Class
	Term Identification
	Credit Hours Attempted
	Credit Hours Attempted for Which
	  Grades Were Received
	Credit Hours Successfully Completed
	Grade Point Average
	Credit Hours Attempted for Non-
	  remedial Classes
	Credit Hours for Which Grades Were
	  Received for Non-remedial Classes
	Credit Hours Successfully Completed for
	  Non-remedial Classes
	Grade Point Average for Non-remedial
	  Classes
	Academic Standing (good, probation,
	  suspension)
	Remediation Attempted
	    reading
	    writing
	    computation
	Remediation Attained
	    reading
	    writing
	    computation
	Program Enrolled In
	Degree/Certificate Awarded
	GED Activity in Term
	ESL Activity in Term
	Term Non-credit Activity
		Transcripts Requested
		Transferred to Another Institution
		Credit Hours Accepted by Transfer
		  Institution
		First-term Enrolled in Transfer
		  Institution
		Program Enrolled at Transfer
		  Institution
		First Degree Attained at Transfer
		  Institution
		Program of Degree Awarded
		Employment Status at Time of
		  Follow-up
		Employment in Field for Which
		  Trained
		Average Hourly Wage
		Employer Ratings
		    technical knowledge
		    work attitude
		    work quality

Source: Ewell, Parker, and Jones, 1988. (See Appendix A for more details.)

to compare term-by-term student progress against many attributes, including age, ethnicity, physical disability, economic disadvantagement, academic ability, and educational background. Besides specifying the data elements, the LONESTAR model provides operational definitions for each, drawing upon several sources, including the Texas Educational Data System; the U.S. Department of Education's Integrated Postsecondary Education Data System; the Higher Education General Information Survey; the Council on Postsecondary Accreditation; the National Center for Education Statistics; and the National Center for Higher Education Management Systems.

The LONESTAR implementation manual specifies a three-step process, illustrated in Figure Fifteen, for constructing the data base. The process presupposes that all student records include a common identification number for each individual (usually the social security number), thus making it possible to merge student files from different data bases. Required data are extracted from existing student records in different college offices, recoded if necessary, and placed into "source files." As the NCHEMS staff explains, "each source file contains the data elements specific to a given portion of the student longitudinal enrollment record. Furthermore, each source file is generally keyed to a single location in the institution's master student record system" (Ewell, Parker, and Jones, 1988, p. 46). Next, data for specific cohorts are downloaded to create or update the longitudinal cohort files. Like the Arapahoe model, the LONESTAR system assumes that updates will occur at two points in each term: (1) a "beginning-of-term" update, just after the college's official reporting or census date, which captures such elements as credit hours attempted, student's academic standing, and student's program of study; and (2) an "end-of-term" update containing data for credit hours successfully completed, grade point average earned, etc. The final step, often omitted from other discussions of student tracking, involves using the cohort files to generate required reports and ad hoc analyses (Figure Sixteen provides an example). These reports take the form of cross-tabulations that compare indicators of academic progress for students with different attributes.

Besides providing a detailed description of the construction of the LONESTAR data base, the NCHEMS staff discuss its interpretation, providing sound advice for any college using indicators to assess student progress. Noting data limitations, Ewell, Parker, and Jones (1988) suggest several guidelines (pp. 101-102), including the following:

- Use the data as indicators to suggest further avenues of inquiry, not as direct measures to be used in making summary judgments;

- Recognize that some persistence indicators are not mutually exclusive — for example a "student may appear in both a completed and a still attending category, because of reenrollment, after graduation" (p. 102);

- Recognize that many reports generated from the data base provide snapshot pictures of a cohort at specific points in time — thus, the inclusion of a given student in the "drop-out" or "first-term-only" categories is provisional and may change in subsequent terms as the student stops in and out of the institution;

- To reduce the likelihood of misinterpreting data, analyze progress indicators against multiple variables — for example, "If a given Progress Report indicates that a particular student population contains a substantial proportion of starters still enrolled, this may be because average loads are quite low, and not because students in the population are encountering academic difficulty" (p. 102).

- Recognize that small cell sizes (n's) may produce spurious results, thus limiting the degree to which data can be broken down for analysis.

FIGURE FIFTEEN

Basic Procedures for Creating Longitudinal Tracking Files

I. Extract Student Data from College Files and Other Sources

Student Records	Assessment Center	Feedback from 4-year Colleges	Research Office

II. Download Fields and Recode as Necessary into Source File

	SSN	Cohort
Student A		F 87
Student B		S 88
Student C		F 88
Student D		S 89
o		
o		
Student ZZZ		F 89

III. Add to Cohort Files

Term Since Entry

Cohort	1	2	3	4	5
Students Entering in Fall '87					X
Students Entering in Spring '88				X	
Students Entering in Fall '88			X		
Students Entering in Spring '89		X			
Students Entering in Fall '89	X				

FIGURE SIXTEEN

Examples of Progress Report Generated by LONESTAR for XXXXXXXXX Cohort as of XXXXXXXXX Term By Optional Demographic Elements

	Total Students	Enrolled	Not Enrolled	Dropped Out	Suspended/ Dismissed	Completers	First Term Only	Re-enrolled Completers
Number of Dependents: 0 1-4 5 or more								
Special Populations: Active Military Incarcerated Other								
Dependency Status: Independent Dependent								
Physical Disabilities: Deaf Deaf-Blind Hard of Hearing Orthopedically Impaired Other Health Impaired Speech Impaired Visually Handi-capped								

Source: Ewell, Parker, and Jones, 1988, p.67.

AACJC —FIPSE Model

In October 1988 AACJC convened a panel of experts to suggest the components of a model student tracking system for community, technical, and junior colleges. At the meeting, the panel members drew heavily upon the LONESTAR effort, and the tentative model suggested by the panel bears a strong resemblance to the LONESTAR data base. For example, the data elements in the model, outlined in Figure Seventeen, include placement scores on math, reading, and writing tests as student attributes against which outcomes can be measured. The model also calls for the inclusion of term-by-term indicators of the performance of students in remedial classes. This emphasis on basic skills testing and remediation reflects the great concern community college educators have for documenting their success with students who are ill-prepared for college-level work.

The remaining variables in the model are familiar components of community college student flow research, tying the attributes that students bring with them to the college to indicators of (1) term-by-term progress and (2) educational and employment success after leaving the college. Appendix Two provides a detailed look at the model, outlining not only the data elements, but the suggestions that panel members had for framing survey questions as well. In general, the model is less extensive than the LONESTAR data base and is meant as a basic system that can be adopted or extended as needed by individual colleges. Nonetheless, it is quite large in comparison to the simplified model proposed by Voorhees and Hart (1989).

FIGURE SEVENTEEN		
Sample Data Elements: AACJC Student Tracking Model		
Student Attributes (collected at student entrance)	Student Progress (collected on a term-by-term basis)	Student Follow-Up (collected after student leaves the college)

ID number (social security no.)
Date of birth
Ethnicity
Address or zip code
English as native language
Last school/college attended
Highest level of schooling attained
Primary reason for attending *this* college at *this* time
Degree goal at *this* institution
Student major subject area
Reading, writing, math placement scores
	Information to be changed as necessary:
	    Address or zip code
	    Degree goal at *this* college
	    Primary reason for attending
	    Declared major
	No. of college-level credits attempted
	No. of college-level credits completed
	GPA for term
	Cumulative GPA
	No. of remedial credits attempted
	No. of remedial credits earned
	Credential earned (if necessary)
	Cumulative credits earned
		Primary reason for enrolling at this college
		Was primary objective attained in the student's opinion?
		Current employment status
		Relationship of job to college studies
		Salary
		Hours per week employed
		Currently enrolled in college?
		    where
		    major field of study
		Number of credit hours currently enrolled in
		    credit hours lost in transfer
		    GPA at new institution

Issues in the Development of Tracking Systems

Despite the growing attention paid to student tracking systems, available literature provides relatively little guidance beyond the basic design and construction of student tracking systems. Examination of these designs reveals tracking systems as promising research tools that replace ad hoc longitudinal studies with a centralized and on-going data collection system providing indicators of student progress over time. Such systems also take full advantage of data base software packages that generate cross-tabulations comparing outcomes against numerous student attribute variables, including demographic characteristics and academic ability. But the success of these systems will depend on the ability of colleges to implement and use them, making the tracking system a regular part of the college's data collection and institutional review procedures. Several inter-related issues, outlined below, are central to this implementation process and should be addressed within the context of each college's unique institutional environment.

Merging Data Files

Ewell, Parker, and Jones point out that "the decision to construct a [tracking] system . . . recognizes that much of the data required to answer questions of institutional effectiveness already reside in institutional data files. The major task is to organize it in ways that will allow for appropriate analysis and reporting" (p. 1). The tracking systems reviewed here, including LONESTAR and the related AACJC model, assume that this organization can be accomplished by merging different student data bases that include a common student identification number for each student. Some data may have to be rekeyed and recoded, however, if common student identification numbers are not used, if the computers used by different campus offices are not compatible, or if data in some files are kept manually.

Centralization

While individual campus offices will continue to collect data for their own purposes, there will have to be some coordination so that data are collected with an eye toward increasing available information about students and their educational progress. This may cause problems. For example, many colleges do not routinely require entering students to specify their educational goals, thus limiting the ability of researchers to correlate student outcomes with student objectives. In these cases, researchers starting a tracking system may request that students be asked about their goals during the registration process. This may be opposed by admissions officials who want to make registration as convenient for students as possible. To avoid conflict, all parties should be involved in planning the tracking system and the procedures for its implementation. Eastern New Mexico State University's planning experience described earlier provides a replicable model involving institutional researchers, the registrar's office, faculty, and other members of the campus community in planning the tracking system.

Marketing Vs. Data Collection

The reluctance of some college officials to collect more data from students or otherwise lengthen the registration process points to a potential conflict between the student tracking concept and college marketing efforts. After making admissions and registration as easy as possible in an effort to attract broader segments of the population, community colleges now face growing demands for information on their students and on college success in helping students advance up the educational pipeline, enter the labor market, or meet other educational goals. The establishment of tracking systems may involve a trade-off at some institutions; an improved information base on students and their progress will be developed at the cost of a lengthened registration process that incorporates procedures for assessing student goals and abilities at entrance. Those building student tracking systems may have to convince the college community of the benefits of this trade-off, explaining that by monitoring student progress and improving institutional practices accordingly, students will be better served in the long run.

A related problem lies in the trade-off that often crops up between research questions on the one hand and the availability of data on the other. Ideally, a tracking system begins with the question, "What indicators of student progress should we collect to help assess institutional effectiveness?" Data collection policies should then follow accordingly. In practice, however, researchers will often begin with the data in hand, asking first "What data are currently available?" and then organizing those data (such as student grades and enrollment patterns) in ways that shed light on student flow. The latter approach will help answer many questions and is preferable to no tracking system at all. In addition, colleges will probably find that most of their research questions can be answered by available data once they are brought together in a tracking system. But as colleges gain experience in student tracking research, they may find that data collection policies need to be changed or augmented to address the student outcomes issues that current institutional research practices were not designed to meet.

Matriculation

In addressing the question, "which students shall be tracked?" colleges in effect ask the question "which students shall we consider to be matriculated?" That is, the college needs to determine which students merit the expenditure involved in term-by-term tracking. Some colleges, noting their open-door philosophy, may want to include all students entering the college at a particular point in time, even those students who will enroll for only one semester. Other colleges may limit the tracking effort to those who have matriculated in a more traditional sense, indicating, either by word or deed, that they will complete a program of study. While it is useful to determine the proportion of entering students who enroll on an ad hoc basis, budget limitations may force colleges to separate these ad hoc students from those who are committed to a program of study. Political pressures may also come into play. Matriculation processes such as those instituted by Miami-Dade Community College or recommended by the state of California may become more common at community colleges as policy makers demand that educators track student progress and take responsibility for student outcomes. A college that claims to do all things for all students can be held accountable for everything or nothing; the former sets the college up for failure, the latter is politically untenable.

Tracking Students After They Leave College

Can student experiences in the workplace and at senior institutions be included in longitudinal student tracking data bases? Ideally, the answer is yes; assessment of student goal attainment requires indicators of the transfer rate of those who enrolled with the intention of preparing for transfer to four-year colleges as well as information on the job placement success of those who enroll with the intention of preparing for a new career. It is for this reason that the AACJC tracking model, outlined in Appendix Two, calls for the integration of follow-up survey data into the tracking system. The model assumes that follow-up questionnaires sent to graduates or non-returning students will include each student's social security number, thus allowing the college to add information on transfer, job placement, and other outcomes to each student record in the data base. Each record, therefore, will include (1) student attribute information that is collected at entrance, (2) term-by-term indicators of student progress while he or she is enrolled at the college, and (3) indicators of employment and educational outcomes after the student leaves the college or graduates.(Follow-up surveys, however, are not always required, especially when gathering data on transfer. Many baccalaureate-granting institutions, often following state mandates, supply community colleges with computer tapes that contain the upper-division records of transfer students. This is a relatively easy procedure; the four-year college need only match its student records against the social security numbers of former community college students.)

The LONESTAR student tracking model, on the other hand, includes follow-up information only as optional data elements, perhaps reflecting the fact that many community colleges find it difficult to longitudinally follow student progress in the workplace or at senior institutions. Besides the methodological problems posed by student follow-up studies, which are expensive to conduct and which often yield low response rates, it takes an inordinately long period of time to assess—on a longitudinal basis—transfer and employment outcomes. Many years may elapse between the time of initial enrollment at the community college and the time a student enrolls in a four-year college or obtains a job. Pressed for information that does not take so long to acquire, institutional researchers may abandon the longitudinal approach in favor of follow-up studies that ask graduates and non-returning students to (1) indicate the reason they initially enrolled in the community college and (2) provide information on their employment and educational experiences after leaving the college. This provides an indication of the degree to which students feel that their goals have been met.

In the final analysis, then, longitudinal student tracking systems following student progress through the institution may have to be supplemented with cross-sectional studies of post-community college experiences to yield indicators of long-term employment and transfer outcomes. In addition to one-shot follow-up surveys, many other approaches to this combination of cross-sectional and longitudinal designs might be undertaken. For example, if a community college receives information from neighboring four-year colleges about former students who have transferred, it may develop trend indicators along the lines of those outlined in Table Seven. While these indicators are not the product of longitudinal student cohort studies, they do shed light on transfer through simple indicators of (1) the number of students entering the community college each year with the intention of transferring, (2) the number of former community college students who show up each year at neighboring four-year colleges, and (3) the number of former community college students receiving bachelor's degrees each year from those four-year institutions. Such indicators do not directly answer the question, "What is the transfer rate of those who enroll with the intention of transferring?" But they do provide a basis for determining—in light of the goals of entering students—whether transfer is increasing or decreasing over time. Those building student tracking systems need to weigh the disadvantages of these cross-sectional supplements (i.e., the information potentially lost by abandoning the longitudinal design) against the benefits of more timely information gained at a lower cost.

TABLE SEVEN					
Cross-Sectional Transfer Indicators for a Hypothetical Community College					
	1984-85	1985-86	1986-87	1987-88	1988-89
No. of First-Time Students Enrolling in the Community College with the Intention of Preparing for Transfer	1000	1010	1020	1003	950
No. of Former Community College Students who Enroll for the First Time in Neighboring Four-Year Colleges	200	199	230	205	210
No. of Former Community College Students who Receive Bachelor's Degrees from Neighboring Four-Year Colleges	170	165	171	180	150

Assessing Student Educational Objectives

A key premise of both the LONESTAR and AACJC models is that student outcomes ought to be assessed in light of student educational objectives. Thus, both models assume that student goals will be determined at entrance and during each term the student is enrolled. This holds out the potential for a more accurate picture of the degree to which students successfully transfer, find new jobs, or otherwise meet their objectives.

But because a student's goal may change from term to term, researchers need to be aware of the limitations of tying data on student goals to data on student outcomes. For example, transfer rates might be based on the experiences of students who initially enroll with the stated intention of preparing for transfer. In this case the transfer rate would be calculated as the percentage of those students who transferred within x number of years; the tendency of some students to change their goals after entering the community college would not be figured into the equation. Thus, any mathematical calculation tying outcomes to initial goals can only be viewed as an indicator that needs to be assessed in light of the degree to which student goals evolve and change as students progress through the community college.

Another limitation lies in the interpretation of student-reported goals and in the questions used to assess them. It is essential that researchers understand the difference between hypothetical questions concerning long-term aspirations and questions concerning immediate educational plans. Asking "What is the highest degree you plan to obtain?" gets at the former, while asking, "What is your primary reason for enrolling at *this* college at *this* time?" gets at the latter. Which question should be used for gathering baseline indicators of student goals? Community college critics often prefer measures of aspiration, noting the discrepancy between the majority of community college students who aspire to baccalaureate or higher degrees and the relatively small number who eventually transfer to four-year colleges. On the other hand, institutional defenders of the community college often prefer measures of immediate educational goals; most students have job-related goals, the defenders claim, and these students have not enrolled with the intention of preparing for transfer to a baccalaureate-granting institution. To minimize the potential misuse of data — which can be interpreted in many ways to suit varying political agendas— those building student tracking systems might want to use *both* aspirations and immediate goals, stressing the limitations of these measures as indicators. A primary tenet of student tracking research is that multiple measures are to be used wherever possible.

Tying the Data Base to Institutional Improvement

Data collection, often viewed by college personnel as an onerous task imposed by outside authorities, sometimes becomes a gratuitous exercise carried out anonymously by institutional research offices; the resulting data reports are duly filed with the appropriate state office or accrediting agency and then forgotten. The success of student tracking systems will in part depend on the ability of institutional researchers to avoid this trap, making sure that data generated by the system are actually used in discussions of institutional improvement. Planning for the use of the data base is as important as seeing to the technical considerations of data collection and data design.

Several factors will encourage the utilization of student tracking systems. Instilling a sense of ownership is an important consideration. When the tracking system is planned by a broad spectrum of the college community and built around questions of interest to faculty and administrators, the information generated by the system stands an excellent chance of being put to use. Another method of fostering this sense of ownership is to report, where possible, data on student progress by program area. It is for this reason that the LONESTAR and AACJC models require students to report their major areas of study. Those most familiar with student tracking systems indicate that unless student goals, performance, and follow-up information can be linked back to the major or program in which the student is or was enrolled, community college faculty and program staff cannot use the tracking information to improve their particular programs.

A second factor contributing to the positive use of student tracking systems is fair and accurate reporting. Guidelines established by the Maryland State Board for Community Colleges for its annual performance profile set an example, carefully noting that performance indicators are not absolute measures designed to rank-order or punish individual programs or colleges (see pages 31-33 of this monograph). College staff should know that the data generated by the student tracking system will be used positively to improve practice and not punitively to pit one program against the other. Indeed, the punitive use of these data makes little sense. For example, if the tracking system determines that x percent of the students in program y achieve their stated educational goals, who is to say that this reflects well or poorly on program y? The purpose of the tracking system is thwarted when the question, "How can we increase student goal attainment?" is replaced by the arbitrary question, "Has a sufficient proportion of students achieved their goals?"

Ample distribution of the reports generated by the tracking system will also be necessary if the system is to be put to use. Simple cross-tabulations, such as the example in Figure Sixteen in this chapter, can do much to pique interest in the tracking system and in what it reveals about student progress and success. While the institutional researcher may be tempted to generate complex reports utilizing inferential statistics to identify correlates of persistence and degree attainment, one-page reports issued periodically with a cross-tabulation and explanatory notes will appeal to a wider audience. This has been demonstrated at the Los Rios Community College District, which disaggregates the findings of student surveys by department and distributes customized reports to department heads and faculty. Unless deans, department heads, and faculty have a chance to review the data—and find in them potential problem areas that bear further investigation—the tracking system will not inform discussions of institutional improvement. Ewell, Parker, and Jones (1988) discuss the generation of cross-tabulations from the data collected in student tracking systems and provide several examples from the LONESTAR system.

Finally, it is important for the college to recognize the limitations of the tracking system and the data it generates. While the tracking system will shed light on student enrollment and degree attainment patterns, suggesting where students apparently succeed and where they apparently do not, the system will not fully explain these patterns. The tracking system might determine, for example, that students entering in year x were less likely to achieve their stated educational goals than students entering in year y. Any number of factors might account for this finding, including differences in the make-up of the two cohorts themselves and changes over time in institutional practices or instruction. Only further investigation will get at the "why" of what the tracking system reveals about student progress over time.

Conclusion

As a theoretical issue, student outcomes assessment has come to the fore, spurred by legislative interest and the demands of accrediting agencies. Many insist that the current interest in outcomes assessment, unlike educational issues that have come and gone in the past, is here to stay. The final verdict, however, awaits further evidence that colleges can sustain the requisite data collection and research efforts.

At many institutions, community college experience with longitudinal research in general and student tracking systems in particular has been quite limited. Because of the focus on compliance reporting requirements, which place a heavy enough burden on college resources, current data collection practices often provide little insight into student flow and outcomes. This is reflected in the literature, which yields few institutionally based longitudinal studies of student progress. It is also reflected in the sometimes ill-informed nature of policy debates concerning institutional effectiveness. How successful are community college educators in preparing students for entry into the labor market? To what extent do remedial programs adequately prepare students for college-level work? Do community colleges have a negative impact on transfer rates and baccalaureate attainment, as some critics charge? Despite the examples of institutional research and data collection cited in this monograph, those attempting to answer these questions often rely on anecdotal evidence.

To be sure, no tracking system will provide definitive answers to questions based on the subjective premises of "adequacy" or "success." In addition, the total picture of institutional effectiveness cannot be reduced to the few and limited indicators around which student tracking systems are built, and some will argue that tracking systems represent an exercise in reduction that does an injustice to the broad scope of the community college mission. Indeed, tracking systems, as they have been discussed here, say nothing about the college role in economic development or non-credit continuing education. But however limited they may at first seem, indicators of the degree to which students meet their educational goals over time are much more telling of the community college story than currently available data on fall headcount enrollments or on the number of associate degrees awarded annually. Without an improved empirical base founded on research programs in which longitudinal studies are the norm rather than the exception, student flow at the community college will remain a black-box phenomenon subject to political interpretations of questionable validity.

APPENDIX ONE:

DATA ELEMENTS IN THE LONESTAR STUDENT TRACKING SYSTEM

Reprinted with permission from *Establishing A Longitudinal Student Tracking System: An Implementation Handbook*, by Peter T. Ewell, Ronald Parker, and Dennis P. Jones (Boulder, Colorado: National Center for Higher Education Management Systems, 1988).

DATA ELEMENTS USED IN THE LONESTAR SYSTEM

A. Demographics

Required

1. **Student Identification Number.** Social security number of the student. The institution will assign a unique nine-digit identification number to each student without a social security number.

2. **Gender.** The gender of the student.
    a. **Male.**
    b. **Female.**

3. **Date of Birth.** The last two digits of the year, month, and day of the birth of the student (YYMMDD).

4. **Race/Ethnic Identification.** Categories used to describe groups to which individuals belong, identify with, or belong in the eyes of the community. The categories do not denote scientific definitions of anthropological origins. A person may be counted in only one group.

    a. **White, Non-Hispanic.** A person having origins in any of the original peoples of Europe, North Africa, or the Middle East.
    b. **Black, Non-Hispanic.** A person having origins in any of the Black racial groups of Africa.
    c. **Hispanic.** A person of Mexican, Puerto Rican, Cuban, Central or South American, or other Spanish culture or origin, regardless of race.
    d. **Asian or Pacific Islander.** A person having origins in any of the original peoples of the Far East, Southeast Asia, the Indian Subcontinent, or Pacific Islands.
    e. **American Indian or Alaskan Native.** A person having origins in any of the original peoples of North America who maintains cultural identification through tribal affiliation and community recognition.
    f. **Non-resident Alien.** A person who is not a citizen or national of the United States and who is in this country on a visa or temporary basis and does not have the right to remain indefinitely.

5. **Citizenship.** The citizenship classification of a student at time of entry to the institution.

    a. **United States Citizen.**
    b. **Foreign National.** A citizen of a country other than the United States.

        (1) **Non-resident Alien.** A person who is not a citizen or national of the United States and who is in this country on a visa or temporary basis and does not have the right to remain indefinitely.
        (2) **Resident Alien.** Non-citizens who have been lawfully admitted to the United States for permanent residence and who hold a "green card" (Form I-151).

6. **Residence at Time of Entry.** The officially recognized residence of a student at the time of first admission to the institution. Typically, this will be determined by the student's tuition classification or other registration records. Students who are resident or non-resident aliens will retain a "foreign" designation regardless of whether they have a local address.

   a. **In-District.** Students legally domiciled within the district of the postsecondary institution at the time of first admission to the institution.
   b. **In-State.** Students legally domiciled in Texas but out of the district at the time of first admission.
   c. **Out-of-State.** Students legally domiciled in a state other than Texas at the time of first admission. (Foreign students are not included in this category.)
   d. **Foreign.** Students legally domiciled in a country other than the United States at the time of first admission.

7. **Physical Disabilities.** Students evaluated as having any one of the following impairments, who because of those impairments need special education and related services.

   a. **Deaf.** A hearing impairment so severe that the student is hindered in processing linguistic information through hearing, with or without amplification, which adversely affects educational performance.
   b. **Deaf-Blind.** Concomitant hearing and visual impairments, the combination of which causes such severe communication and other developmental and educational problems that they cannot be accommodated in special education programs solely for deaf or blind students.
   c. **Hard of Hearing.** A hearing impairment, whether permanent or fluctuating, that adversely affects a student's educational performance but which is not included under the definition of deaf.
   d. **Orthopedically Impaired.** A severe orthopedic impairment that adversely affects a student's educational performance. The term includes impairment caused by congenital anomaly, disease, and from other causes.
   e. **Other Health Impaired.** Limited strength, vitality, or alertness, due to chronic or acute health problems such as a heart condition, tuberculosis, rheumatic fever, nephritis, asthma, sickle cell anemia, hemophilia, epilepsy, lead poisoning, leukemia, or diabetes, that adversely affects a student's educational performance.
   f. **Speech Impaired.** A communication disorder, such as stuttering, impaired articulation, a language impairment, or a voice impairment, that adversely affects a student's educational performance.
   g. **Visually Handicapped.** A visual impairment that, even with correction, adversely affects a student's educational performance.

8. **Learning Disability.** A disorder in one or more of the basic psychological processes involved in understanding or in using spoken or written language, which may manifest itself in an imperfect ability to listen, think, speak, read, write, spell, or do mathematical calculations. The term includes such conditions as perceptual handicaps, brain injury, minimal brain dysfunction, dyslexia, and developmental aphasia. The term does not include students who have learning problems that are primarily the result of visual, hearing, or motor handicaps, of mental retardation, or of environmental, cultural, or economic disadvantage.

9. **Economically Disadvantaged.** A student whose family income is at or below the national poverty level; a student (or parents) who is unemployed, on public assistance, or is institutionalized or under state guardianship and who requires special services, assistance, or programs in order to enable that person to succeed in a vocational program. This is a self-reported item historically collected only for occupational students.

10. **Academically Disadvantaged.** A student who lacks reading skills, writing skills, mathematical skills, or who performs below grade level and who requires special services, assistance, or programs in order to succeed in a vocational program. This is a self-reported item historically collected only for occupational students.

11. **Current Employment.** Describes the current employment situation of the student.

    a.   **Employed Full-Time.** Employed for 35 hours per week or more.
    b.   **Employed Part-Time.** Employed for less than 35 hours per week.
    c.   **Employed as a Homemaker.**
    d.   **Not Employed, Seeking Work.**
    e.   **Not Employed, Not Seeking Work.**

Optional

1. **Zip Code.** Five-digit code that identifies each postal delivery area in the United States.

2. **Highest Level of Education Obtained by Father.** Describes the highest level of formal education obtained by the student's father.

    a.   **Not a High School Graduate.**
    b.   **High School Graduate.**
    c.   **Some College or Associate Degree.**
    d.   **Bachelor's Degree or Above.**

3. **Highest Level of Education Obtained by Mother.** Describes the highest level of formal education obtained by the student's mother.

    a.   **Not a High School Graduate.**
    b.   **High School Graduate.**
    c.   **Some College or Associate Degree.**
    d.   **Bachelor's Degree or Above.**

4. **Marital Status.** Describes the marital status of the student at time of entry.

    a.   **Single, Never Married.**
    b.   **Married.**
    c.   **Divorced/Separated.**
    d.   **Widow/Widower.**

5. **Number of Dependents.** The number of dependents supported by the student at time of entry.

6. **Special Populations.** The student's membership in an identified population relevant to attending a postsecondary institution.

      a.   **Active Military.**
      b.   **Incarcerated.**
      c.   **Other.**

7. **Dependency Status.** The status of the student with respect to financial support at time of admission.

      a.   **Independent.** A student who is 24 or older by December 31 of the award year, who is an orphan, ward of the court, a veteran of the Armed Forces, or has legal dependents other than a spouse; or is a married student who will not be claimed as a dependent for income tax purposes by a parent or guardian for the first calendar year of the award year, and who, if treated as an independent student in the preceding award year, was not claimed for income tax purposes by anyone other than a spouse for the first calendar year of that award year; who is a single undergraduate student with no dependents who was not claimed as a dependent by a parent or guardian for income tax purposes for the two calendar years preceding the award year and demonstrated total self-sufficiency during the two calendar years preceding the award year in which the initial award will be granted by demonstrating an annual total income of $4,000; or who is a student for whom a financial aid administrator makes a documented determination of independence by reason of other unusual circumstances.

      b.   **Dependent.** Any student who does not meet the criteria for designation as an independent student.

B. Educational Background

Required

1. **Last High School Attended.** The 9-digit College Board classification is recommended. Out-of-state schools will typically be assigned a single code. Institutions have the option of using their own codes.

2. **Type of High School Award.** The type of award granted to the student on completion of a high school curriculum.

      a.   **Standard.**
      b.   **Collegiate.**
      c.   **Honors.**
      d.   **Certificate of Attendance.**
      e.   **GED.**
      f.   **No High School Award.**

3. **Date of High School Diploma or Its Equivalent.** Month and the last two digits of the year of

the receipt of the student's high school diploma or its equivalent (YYMM).

4.   **High School Grade Point Average.** Grade point average earned in high school, typically on a scale based on 100.

5.   **Last College Attended.** The 6-digit Federal Interagency Commission on Education (FICE) number assigned by the Department of Education is preferred.

6.   **Previous College-Level Academic Experience.** The extent of past postsecondary educational experience obtained prior to enrollment at the college.

    a.   **None.**
    b.   **Some Postsecondary Education.** Attendance at a postsecondary educational institution not resulting in a degree or certificate.
    c.   **Postsecondary Award, Certificate, or Diploma.** An award granted for the completion of an organized program of study at the postsecondary level of instruction (typically at least one, but less than two, full-time equivalent academic years) resulting in a certificate or equivalent award.
    d.   **Associate Degree.** An award granted on completion of an educational program that is not of a baccalaureate level and that normally requires at least two but less than four years of full-time equivalent college work.
    e.   **Bachelor's Degree.** An award granted on completion of an educational program that normally requires at least four, but not more than five, years of full-time equivalent college-level work. This includes all bachelor's degrees conferred in a cooperative or work-study plan or program.
    f.   **Master's Degree.** An award granted on completion of a program of study of at least the full-time equivalent of one, but not more than two, academic years of work beyond the bachelor's degree.
    g.   **Doctor's Degree.** An award granted on completion of a program of study at the graduate level that terminates in a doctor's degree. The doctor's degree classification includes such degrees as doctor of education, doctor of juridical science, doctor of public health, and the Ph.D. in any field whether agronomy, education, opthamology, etc.
    h.   **First-Professional Degree.** An award granted on completion of the following: (1) the academic requirements to begin practice in the profession; (2) at least two years of college work prior to entrance to the program; and (3) a total of at least six academic years of college work to complete the degree program, including prior required college work plus the length of the professional program itself. Includes chiropractic, general dentistry, general medicine, optometry, osteopathic medicine, pharmacy, podiatry, veterinary medicine, law, and theological studies.

7.   **Remediation Status at Time of Entry—Reading.** The assessed level of student proficiency in reading determined by the institution for purposes of placement and remediation. Locally defined and locally supplied category with seven levels available for local assignment.

8.   **Remediation Status at Time of Entry—Writing.** The assessed level of student proficiency in

writing determined by the institution for purposes of placement and remediation. Locally defined and locally supplied category with seven levels available for local assignment.

9.   **Remediation Status at Time of Entry—Computation.** The assessed level of student proficiency in computation determined by the institution for purposes of placement and remediation. Locally defined and locally supplied category with seven levels available for local assignment.

10.   **Limited English Speaking Proficiency.** A student is in this class if he or she does not speak and understand the English language in an instructional setting well enough to benefit from the instruction and complete the objectives of the program without special assistance.

Optional

1.   **High School Rank.** The rank of a student in his or her high school graduating class.

2.   **Size of High School Graduating Class.** Number of students in a student's high school graduating class.

3.   **High School Track.** The area of concentration in which high school students take most of their coursework.

        a.   **Standard.** A program of studies designed to prepare students for common activities as citizens, family members, and workers. A standard program of studies may include instruction in both academic and vocational areas.

        b.   **Collegiate.** A program of studies for students who have achieved a high standard of performance in a special subject area or who have generally high scholarship.

        c.   **Honors.** A program of studies for students who have achieved a high standard of performance in a special subject area or who have generally high scholarship.

4.   **Hours Transferred for Credit.** Number of credit hours in approved college-level courses that the institution accepts for transfer credit.

5.   **Initial Performance on Local Proficiency Exam—Reading.** Raw scores attained by the student in an initial administration of the proficiency exam in reading.

6.   **Initial Performance on Local Proficiency Exam—Writing.** Raw score attained by the student in an initial administration of a proficiency exam in writing.

7.   **Initial Performance on Local Proficiency Exam—Computation.** Raw score attained by the student in an initial administration of a proficiency exam in computation.

8.   **Initial Performance on State-Mandated Proficiency Exam—Reading.** Raw score attained by the student in an initial administration of the state-mandated proficiency exam in reading.

9.   **Initial Performance on State-Mandated Proficiency Exam—Writing.** Raw score attained by the student in an initial administration of the state-mandated proficiency exam in writing.

10. **Initial Performance on State-Mandated Proficiency Exam—Computation.** Raw score attained by the student in an initial administration of the state-mandated proficiency exam in computation.

C. Enrollment Status

<u>Required</u>

1. **First Term of Academic History.** The term and the last two digits of the year the student is first enrolled at the institution (YYT). Terms are coded.

   a. **Fall.** First term of the academic year.
   b. **Spring.** Second term of the academic year.
   c. **Summer I.** First term of the summer session.
   d. **Summer II.** Second term of the summer session.

2. **Admission Status.** The type of admission to the institution granted to the student on initial entry.

   a. **Full.**
   b. **Provisional or Restricted.**

3. **Basis of Admission.** The basis on which the decision to admit the student was taken.

   a. **High School Graduate.**
   b. **Individual Approval.** Student's application is approved by the institution on a case-by-case basis.
   c. **General Education Development (GED) Certificate.**
   d. **College Transfer.**
   e. **Transient.** Student is enrolled formally in another institution and is not seeking a degree.
   f. **Readmission, Previously Enrolled.** Student is readmitted to the institution after an absence of six or more years.
   g. **Early Admission—Concurrent Enrollment.** The student is admitted and receiving college credit while still in high school.
   h. **Other.**

4. **Financial Aid Status.** The status of the student with respect to financial aid upon initial term of admission.

   a. **Applied.** Student made application to receive financial aid.
   b. **Applied, and Determined Eligible.** Student made application and was determined eligible to receive financial aid.
   c. **Applied, Determined Eligible, and Awarded.** Student made application to receive financial aid, was determined eligible, was awarded an amount.
   d. **Applied, Determined Eligible, Awarded, and Collected.** Student made application to receive financial aid, was determined eligible, was awarded an

amount, and collected the award.

    e.   **Did Not Apply.** Student did not apply for financial aid.

5.   **Time of Attendance.** The time of day or week a student predominantly attended class(es).

    a.   **Regular Day Program.**
    b.   **Evening.**
    c.   **Weekend.**
    d.   **Other.**

6.   **Location of Instruction.** The location where the student predominantly attended classes.

    a.   **On-Campus.**
    b.   **Off-Campus.**

7.   **Initial Program at Time of Entry.** The initial program the student enrolled in at the time of entry to the institution. The CES Classification of Instructional Programs (CIP) is recommended.

8.   **Program Track.** The general community college program track in which a student is enrolled.

    a.   **Vocational.** A program of studies designed to prepare students for employment in one or more semi-skilled, skilled, or technical occupations.
    b.   **Academic.** A program of studies designed primarily to prepare students for a four-year college program.
    c.   **Unclassified.** A student who has not formally specified an occupational or academic program track.

9.   **Student Objective in Attending College.** The primary reason a student reports for attending college.

    a.   **Get a Job.**
    b.   **Improve Skills Needed in Current Job.**
    c.   **Get a Better Job.**
    d.   **Earn One-Year Certificate.**
    e.   **Earn Two-Year Degree.**
    f.   **Earn Four-Year Degree.**
    g.   **Personal Enrichment.**
    h.   **Other.**

10.   **Intended Duration.** The amount of time that the student plans to study at the institution from the time of registration.

    a.   **One Term Only.**
    b.   **Two Terms.**
    c.   **One Year.**
    d.   **Two Years.**

        e.   **Three Years.**

        f   **More than Three Years.**

11.   **Term of Enrollment in First College-Level English Course.** The term and the last two digits of the year the student enrolled in his/her first college-level English course at the institution (YYT). Supplied from a designated list of such courses provided by each institution.

        a.   **Fall.** First term of the academic year.

        b.   **Spring.** Second term of the academic year.

        c.   **Summer I.** First term of the summer session.

        d.   **Summer II.** Second term of the summer session.

12.   **Performance in First College-Level English Course.** Grade earned by the student in his/her first completed college-level English course at the institution defined as above.

13.   **Term of Enrollment in First College-Level Math Course.** The term and the last two digits of the year the student enrolled in his/her first college-level math course at the institution (YYT). Supplied from a designated list of such courses provided by the institution.

        a.   **Fall.** First term of the academic year.

        b.   **Spring.** Second term of the academic year.

        c.   **Summer I.** First term of the summer session.

        d.   **Summer II.** Second term of the summer session.

14.   **Performance in First College-Level Math Course.** Grade earned by the student in his/her first college-level math course at the institution defined as above.

Optional

1.   **Type of Financial Aid Award.** The basic type of financial aid awarded on initial entry.

        a.   **Need-Based.**

        b.   **Merit-Based.**

        c.   **Other.**

D. Term Tracking

Required

1.   **Term Identification.** Term to which all of the following elements apply.

        a.   **Fall.** First term of the academic year.

        b.   **Spring.** Second term of the academic year.

        c.   **Summer I.** First term of the summer session.

        d.   **Summer II.** Second term of the summer session.

2.   **Student Credit Hours Attempted as of the Official State Reporting Date.** The total number

of credit hours a student is enrolled in the term of record as of the designated census date for state reporting.

3. **Student Credit Hours Attempted for which Grades Were Received.** The total number of student credit hours actually completed by the student in the term of record.

4. **Student Credit Hours Successfully Completed.** The total number of student credit hours attempted by the student for which a passing grade was received in the term of record.

5. **Grade Point Average.** Typically on a scale of 0.000 to 4.000 with 4.000 = 'A' for credit earned in all coursework.

6. **Student Credit Hours Attempted as of the Official State Reporting Date for Non-remedial Courses.** The total number of credit hours for which a student is enrolled in non-remedial courses in the term of record as of the designated census date for state reporting.

7. **Student Credit Hours Attempted for Which Grades Were Received for Non-remedial Courses.** The total number of student credit hours actually completed in non-remedial courses by the student in the term of record and included in the GPA calculation.

8. **Student Credit Hours for Which the Grade A, B, or C Was Received for Non-remedial Courses.** The total number of student credit hours attempted in non-remedial courses by the student for which the grade A, B, or C was received in the term of record.

9. **Grade Point Average for Non-remedial Courses.** Typically on a scale of 0.000 to 4.000 with 4.000 = 'A' for credit earned in coursework in non-remedial courses only.

10. **Academic Standing.** The official academic standing of the student during the term of record.

    a. **Good Academic Standing.**
    b. **Probation.**
    c. **Suspension.**

11. **Remediation by Level Attempted—Reading.** The level of formal remediation of an assessed deficiency attempted by the student in reading during the term of record. The level should reflect the level of proficiency that the student would have attained if the remediation were successfully completed. If no remediation is attempted during the term, the element is left blank.

12. **Proficiency Level Attained—Reading.** The assessed level of student proficiency in reading determined by the institution for purposes of placement and remediation. Locally defined and locally supplied category.

13. **Remediation by Level Attempted—Writing.** The level of formal remediation of an assessed deficiency attempted by the student in writing during the term of record. The level should reflect the level of proficiency that the student would have attained if the remediation were successfully completed. If no remediation is attempted during the term, the element is left blank.

14. **Proficiency Level Attained—Writing.** The assessed level of student proficiency in writing determined by the institution for purposes of placement and remediation. Locally defined and locally supplied category.

15. **Remediation by Level Attempted—Computation.** The level of formal remediation of an assessed deficiency attempted by the student in computation during the term of record. The level should reflect the level of proficiency that the student would have attained if the remediation were successfully completed. If no remediation is attempted during the term, the element is left blank.

16. **Proficiency Level Attained—Computation.** The assessed level of student proficiency in computation determined by the institution for purposes of placement and remediation. Locally defined and locally supplied category.

17. **Program Enrolled In.** The current program in which the student is enrolled. The CES Classification of Instructional Programs (CIP) is recommended. For programs not included in CIP, a local code is used.

18. **Type of Degree/Certificate Awarded.** The type of award attained, if any, during the term of record.

   a. **None.**
   b. **Postsecondary Awards or Certificates** (less than one year). An award granted for the completion of a program that is completed in less than one academic year (2 semesters or 3 quarters) or less than 900 contact hours by a student enrolled full-time.
   c. **Postsecondary Awards or Certificates** (at least one but less than two academic years of work). An award granted for the completion of an organized program of study at the postsecondary level of instruction of at least one but less than two full-time-equivalent academic years; or designed for completion in at least 30 but less than 60 credit hours, or in at least 900 but less than 1,800 contact hours.
   d. **Academic Associate Degree.** An award granted upon completion of an educational program that is not of a baccalaureate level and that normally requires at least two but less than four years of full-time-equivalent college work and is typically assigned an AA or AS degree.
   e. **Applied Associate Degree.** An award granted on completion of an applied technology program that is not of a baccalaureate level and is typically assigned as an AAS degree.

19. **Term GED Activity.** Indicates whether a student was enrolled in and/or completed a GED program at the institution during the term of record.

   a. **Enrolled in GED Program.**
   b. **Enrolled in and Completed ESL Program.**
   c. **Not Enrolled in GED Program.**

20. **Term ESL Activity.** Indicates whether a student was enrolled in and/or completed an ESL

program at the institution during the term of record.

    a.   **Enrolled in ESL Program.**
    b.   **Enrolled in and Completed ESL Program.**
    c.   **Not Enrolled in ESL Program.**

21.   **Term Non-Credit Activity.** Indicates whether a student was enrolled in and/or completed a non-credit program of study at the institution during the term of record.

    a.   **Enrolled in Non-credit Program.**
    b.   **Enrolled in and Completed Non-credit Program.**
    c.   **Not Enrolled in Non-credit Program.**

Optional

1.   **Honor Points for All Courses.** The numerator for the GPA calculation. Calculated as the sum of products of the number of course credit hours and grade point earned in that course.

2.   **Honor Points for Non-remedial Courses.** The numerator for the GPA calculation for non-remediation courses. Calculated as the sum of products of the number of course credit hours and grade points (0-4) earned in that course.

3.   **Performance on Local Proficiency Exam—Reading.** Raw score attained by the student in a retest of the proficiency exam during the term of record.

4.   **Performance on Local Proficiency Exam—Writing.** Raw score attained by the student in a retest of the proficiency exam during the term record.

5.   **Performance on Local Proficiency Exam—Computation.** Raw score attained by the student in a retest of the proficiency exam during the term record.

6.   **Hours Awarded by Assessment of Learning.** The number of hours earned during the term of record through CLEP, the evaluation of experiential learning, or a similar process.

E. Follow-Up Elements

All Optional

1.   **Transcripts Requested.** One measure that a student is considering transferring to another institution is when the student requests to have transcripts sent to another institution or an employer. To record information on which institution(s), the use of the 6-digit Federal Interagency Commission on Education (FICE) number assigned to the institution by the Department of Education is preferred.

2.   **Transferred to Another Institution.** The 6-digit Federal Interagency Commission on Education

(FICE) number assigned to the institution to which a student has officially transferred by the Department of Education to indicate transfer institution.

3. **Credit Hours Accepted by Transfer Institution.** The number of credit hours earned at this institution that were successfully transferred to another institution.

4. **First Term Enrolled in Transfer Institution.** The term and the last two digits of the year the student is first enrolled at the transfer institution (YYT).

5. **Program Enrolled in at Transfer Institution.** The initial program the student enrolls in at the time of entry to the transfer institution. The CES Classification of Instructional Programs (CIP) is recommended.

6. **First Degree Attained in Transfer Institution.** The first degree attained by a former student at the transfer institution.

7. **Program of Degree Awarded.** The program in which the student receives an award/degree at the transfer institution. The CES Classification of Instructional Programs (CIP) is recommended.

8. **Employment Status at Time of Follow-Up.** The employment status of the student after completion or withdrawal from a program.

   a. **Employed Full-Time.** Employed for 35 hours per week or more.
   b. **Employed Part-Time.** Employed for less than 35 hours per week.
   c. **Employed as Homemaker.**
   d. **Not Employed, Seeking Work.**
   e. **Not Employed, Not Seeking Work.**

9. **Employment in Field for Which Trained.** Student report of the degree to which instruction received is related to current job duties and performance.

   a. **Directly Related.**
   b. **Somewhat Related.**
   c. **Not at All Related.**

10. **Average Hourly Salary/Wage Rate in Current Job.** The current hourly rate of pay reported by the student in his or her current job.

11. **Employer Rating -- Technical Knowledge.** A rating by the current employer of a former student's on-the-job performance with respect to technical knowledge. Computed on a 5-point scale.

12. **Employer Rating -- Work Attitude.** A rating by the current employer of a former student's on-the-job performance with respect to work attitude. Computed on a 5-point scale.

13.   **Employer Rating -- Work Quality.** A rating by the current employer of a former student's on-the-job performance with respect to work quality. Computed on a 5-point scale.

F. Derived Data Elements

While much can be learned from looking at simple demographic or performance variables like gender or GPA, it is often useful to calculate indicators of student behavior. These indicators are derived or inferred from other elements in the student records system by a specific computational or logical algorithm. Examples are:

1.   **Number of Terms Enrolled.** The sum of the number of terms that a student in a particular cohort has attempted to complete courses for one or more hours of credit. Summer terms may or may not be included at user option.

2.   **Dropped Out After One Term.** Student has enrolled for one or more credit hours of instruction during the first term of enrollment but registered for zero hours for each of the other terms being analyzed.

3.   **Total Credit Hours Attempted.** The sum of the credit hours attempted to date.

4.   **Total Credit Hours Completed.** The sum of credit hours successfully completed to date.

5.   **Credit Hours Completion Rate.** Total semester credit hours completed divided by total semester credit hours attempted.

6.   **Average Load.** Total semester credit hours attempted divided by the number of terms with semester hours attempted greater than zero.

7.   **Dropped Out.** Student has not enrolled for two consecutive regular terms or one regular and two summer terms (consecutive).

8.   **Degree Completed.** Student has completed a degree or certificate program.

9.   **Still Attending.** Student is currently enrolled for one or more credit hours.

10.   **Cumulative GPA.** A weighted average of term GPAs for all terms in which a student is enrolled for one or more credit hours.

11.   **Age.** The difference between the year of the term being studied and the student's year of birth.

APPENDIX TWO:

AACJC PROJECT ADVISORY BOARD RECOMMENDATIONS

STUDENT TRACKING MODEL: DATA ELEMENTS

AACJC
PROJECT ADVISORY BOARD RECOMMENDATIONS

STUDENT TRACKING MODEL: DATA ELEMENTS

In October 1988 AACJC convened a panel of experts to suggest possible components of a model student tracking system for community, technical, and junior colleges. The panel included the following individuals:

Donald S. Doucette, Associate Director
League for Innovation in the Community College (California)

Dennis P. Jones, President
National Center for Higher Education Management Systems (Colorado)

Janis Cox Jones (formerly Coffey), Director
Planning and Research
Los Rios Community College District (California)

John Losak
Dean of Institutional Research
Miami-Dade Community College (Florida)

John A. Lucas, Director
Planning and Research
William Rainey Harper Community College (Illinois)

Daniel D. McConochie, Director
Research and Policy Analysis
Maryland State Board for Community Colleges

The suggestions made by the panel are meant as a bare-bones student tracking model that may be adapted or extended as needed by individual colleges. The model assumes that procedures are in place to collect data for each student when he/she enters the college, during the course of his/her studies at the college, and after he/she has left the college. The variables included in the model can be categorized into three groups:

1. Data on the attributes that students bring with them to the colleges, including age, ethnicity, prior educational attainment, current educational goals, intended field of study, and academic ability.

2. Data on the term-by-term progress of the students, including term grade point average (GPA), the ratio of credit hours completed to credit hours attempted, and degree completion (where applicable).

3. Follow-up data on non-returning students and graduates. These data cover the educational and employment status of the students after they leave the college.

Collection of these data allows researchers to assess student flow and goal attainment along any number of variables, including demographics, enrollment status (full-time/part-time), subject area, academic ability, and student educational objectives. Colleges may want to add or delete variables as needed.

The data elements suggested by the panel are outlined below. (An asterisk beside the name of a data element indicates that this variable was considered optional by the advisory panel.)

Data on Student Attributes

Data on student attributes—including demographic characteristics, educational goals, and measures of academic ability—allow researchers to compare educational progress and outcomes for various student groups. Collecting information on the variables outlined below facilitates the tracking of minority students, women, students with varying academic abilities, students with varying educational objectives, students with differing educational backgrounds, and students concentrating in different fields of study. Each college needs to determine the student population that are of particular interest and modify the student tracking system accordingly. For example, if a college needs to compare the educational progress of students who receive financial aid with the educational progress of non-aided students, the college will need to add a variable indicating the amount and type of student financial aid received.

Data Element	Comments
ID Number	Preferably the student's social security number. This is the number that will be used to link student records from various data files. For example, data on Student A's educational objectives may be in a registrar's file, data on his entry test scores may be stored in the student services office, and data on his grades after transferring to a four-year college will be in a file at the prior institution. It is hoped that each of the records in these different files will be tagged with a common ID number.
Date of Birth	Month/Day/Year
Ethnicity	However defined. Categories used by the U.S. Department of Education in its IPEDS surveys are: White, Non-Hispanic, Hispanic; Asian, Pacific Islander; Native American; Black, Non-Hispanic; Non-resident Alien.
Address/Zip Code	This should be updated each term. A current address will be needed for follow-up purposes.
First Term in Which Student Was Enrolled	The student record should include a tag indicating when the student enrolled for the first time. This is necessary for cohort analyses; cohorts are usually defined as those students who enter the college at a particular point.
Last School or College Attended	Name of school or college the student last attended.
Date of Last School/College Attendance	Month and year in which the student left the last school or college attended.

Highest Educational Credential Previously Attained

Suggested categories are:

1. No high school credential, either diploma or GED
2. High school diploma
3. GED
4. Some college, no credential
5. College certificate
6. Associate degree
7. Baccalaureate
8. Master's or higher

Primary Reason for Attending This college at This Time

This is a crucial question because it is important to tie outcomes (such as transfer rates or job obtainment rates) to student intentions. In asking the question, it is important to avoid hypothetical queries that yield spurious results. Too often, students are asked "What is the highest degree you want to obtain?" The results almost always indicate that 75% want to obtain baccalaureate or higher degrees. The advisory board recommended a question that in past surveys has yielded more realistic results: "What is your most important reason for attending this college at this time?" (Choose one):

1. To prepare for transfer to a four-year college or university
2. To gain skills necessary to enter a new occupation
3. To gain skills necessary to retrain, remain current, or advance in a current occupation
4. To satisfy a personal objective
5. To improve basic reading, writing, or math skills

Degree Goal at This Institution

There are several ways to ask this question. One is to ask: "Do you plan to earn an associate degree or certificate at this college?" (Yes, No, Undecided) Another is to ask: "What is the probability that you will obtain an associate degree at this institution within five years?" (Very Likely, Undecided, Not Likely at All).

Major Field of Study

What subject area does the student plan to concentrate on at this college, regardless of educational objectives or degree plans? This will be an important question, allowing colleges to track students in various programs. This type of information should be of interest to faculty, thus making the tracking system of interest to the wider college community, not just top administrators and institutional researchers.

Eligibility to Enroll in College-Level Courses

The advisory panel felt it important to evaluate outcomes against some measure of academic ability, thereby helping to assess the progress of two student groups: those whose academic ability indicates that they are ready for college-level work and those who need remedial assistance. The panel felt that basic skills test scores would be appropriate indicators:

1. Writing placement scores
2. Reading placement scores
3. Math placement scores

*Socioeconomic (SES) Measures

SES measures are problematic. It is very difficult to accurately define socioeconomic status, let alone measure it. At the community college, the problem of assessing SES is made even more difficult because of the college's diverse student population. For example, four-year colleges often measure SES by asking about parental income. But this may hardly be appropriate for older students who are on their own. Asking about self-income is problematic; the self-income of an 18-year-old living with his or her parents may grossly underestimate his or her actual income. The same would be true for a student with a working spouse.

*Disabilities

Colleges may want to tag each student record for disabilities (physical or learning disabilities) where they exist.

*Compelling Influences on the Student's Decision to Attend This Particular College

Many colleges may want to assess the reasons students have for choosing and attending their colleges (convenient location, low cost, availability of a specific program, etc.)

Information to Be Collected and/or Updated on a Term-by-Term Basis

The second component of the student tracking system involves the collection of information for each student in the cohort on a term-by-term basis. These data are collected in an effort to assess the enrollment status of students in each term (part-time/full-time), the degree to which students successfully complete the courses in which they enroll, and the grade point average earned for the term.

In addition, the panel felt that the student tracking system should include indicators of student participation in remedial classes and of the degree to which participating students successfully complete those courses. If this information is collected, colleges can track the subsequent educational progress of students who take remedial classes.

Finally, this component of the tracking system requires researchers to update some of the student attribute information listed above. In particular, name and address changes should be noted, as well as any changes that students make in their degree goals, reasons for enrolling, or intentions to earn a degree at the institution.

Data Element	Comments
Term ID	Each of the data elements listed below needs to be tagged with a term identifier. For example, term GPA should clearly indicate the term of record for that GPA (Fall 1989, Winter 1990, etc.).
Address/Zip Code	This should be updated each term. A current address will be needed for follow-up purposes.

Degree Goal at <u>This</u> Institution

Same question used at the initial assessment of the student's degree goals.

Primary Reason for Attending <u>This</u> Institution at This Time

Same question used at the initial assessment of the student's primary reason for attending. "What is your most important reason for attending this college at this time?" (Choose one):

1. To prepare for transfer to a four-year college or university
2. To gain skills necessary to enter a new occupation
3. To gain skills necessary to retrain, remain current, or advance in a current occupation
4. To satisfy a personal objective
5. To improve basic reading, writing, or math skills.

Major Field of Study

Same question used at the initial assessment of the student's major field of study.

Number of College-level Credit Hours Attempted

At the beginning of the term, how many college-level credits did the student sign up for? If zero, this will be an indication that the student stopped out. This variable is of course also useful in determining whether the student is enrolled on a part-time or full-time basis.

Number of College-Level Credit Hours Successfully Completed

This is meant as a measure of the extent to which students complete classes with a passing grade.

Number of Cumulative College-Level Credits Earned to Date at the End of the Term

Term GPA

Cumulative GPA to Date at the End of the Term

Number of Remedial Course Credits Attempted

Because many colleges will want to assess the progress of students who take remedial courses, the advisory panel felt it necessary to include measures of participation in remedial classes.

Number of Remedial Course Credits Completed

This is meant as a measure of the extent to which students successfully complete remedial classes.

Follow-up Information

Most colleges survey students to follow up on their educational or vocational progress. It is necessary to tie such information to the tracking system in order to answer long-range but crucial outcomes related to transfer and job obtainment.

Two groups of students need to be followed up: graduates (those who complete a degree or certificate); and non-returning students. The question arises: Who is a non-returning student? Each college must supply its own answer. A non-returner might be defined, for example, as a student who does not show up at the college for two or three consecutive terms.

A second question is "How soon after the student leaves the college should a follow-up survey be conducted?" Again, each college needs to make its own determination. In general, a trade-off is involved: the longer the college waits to follow up on graduates or non-returners, the lower the response rate. On the other hand, data collected after a considerable period of time might be more meaningful. The transfer and vocational success of graduates, for example, is best measured a year or two after graduation.

The advisory board recommended that the following data elements be included in follow-up surveys and tied to the student tracking system:

Data Elements	Comments
Primary Reason for Enrolling in the College	A modified version of the question used in the initial assessment of the student's primary reason for enrolling: "What was your primary reason for attending this college?" (Choose one):

1. To prepare for transfer to a four-year college or university
2. To gain skills necessary to enter a new occupation
3. To gain skills necessary to retrain, remain current, or advance in a current occupation
4. To satisfy a personal objective
5. To improve basic reading, writing, or math skills

Even though the student's original and updated "primary reasons for enrolling" are on the student's computer record, asking students again after-the-fact can provide some interesting information, particularly as a cross-check on the "reason for enrolling" statements already on the system.

Student's Perception About the Degree to Which His/Her Objective Has Been Achieved	A simple question could be asked: "To what degree has your educational objective been met?" (Fully, Partially, Not at All).
Student's Current Educational Status	Students should be asked about their current educational status: "Are you enrolled for credit in a school or college?" (Yes, No). If yes, the student might be asked the following:

- Name of the college or school
- Number of credit hours for which the student is currently enrolled
- Major field of study at the college or school
- Credit hours lost in transfer
- Cumulative GPA at the college or school

(Of course, this information collected in student follow-up surveys might well be augmented by data from surrounding four-year colleges, provided these colleges can supply student records that have the appropriate student ID number.

Student's Current Employment Status

The former student should be asked: "Are you currently employed?" (Yes/No). If yes, the respondent should be asked to provide information on the following:

- Number of hours per week currently employed
- Earnings per week (or month or year, as long as a specified time period is employed)
- Relationship of current employment to program of studies at the community college (related, somewhat related, not related at all)

*Student's Perception of His/Her Educational Experience at the Community College

As an option, the college might want to include in the tracking file data on student college evaluations of their community college experience. These data usually derive from survey questions such as "How would you rate the quality of the job training you received at XYZ College?" (Excellent, Good, Fair, Poor).

Further Questions

Besides outlining the components of a student tracking system, the advisory panel addressed additional questions that each college will have to consider as it begins the development of a student tracking data base. These questions are summarized below.

- Which students should be tracked? The advisory board recommends that only students in credit classes should be included in the data base. Beyond that, the college is limited only by the time and resources it wants to devote to the student tracking system. The college may wish to include all those students who enroll for the first time in a particular term (for example, all first-time students enrolling in fall 1989). In starting out, though, the college may want to limit the size of its data base, including (for example) only those enrolled on a full-time basis. Part-time could be included after initial problems in data base construction have been ironed out.

- How will the student data—collected by different departments within the college—be organized into one data base? If student data collected by different college offices are keyed into compatible computer systems utilizing a common ID number for each student, then it should be possible to merge files as needed. Each college will have to assess its situation and merge files accordingly.

- How will the data be used in institutional improvement? It is one thing to collect data, quite another to assure that it will be used in institutional planning and improvement. The advisory board suggests that researchers make a determined effort to educate faculty and staff about the usefulness of the data collected in the student tracking system. If faculty and staff feel the data are valuable, then the data are more likely to be examined and discussed by the broad college community.

REFERENCES

The literature on student tracking is quite limited, focusing more on theoretical considerations than on the more practical questions of data base design and use. The dearth of materials reflects the limited experience community colleges have with student tracking in particular and longitudinal research in general.

Nonetheless, those building student tracking systems should be aware of the few pioneering works that have paved the way for longitudinal research on student outcomes. The work of Peter Ewell (1983, 1987a, 1987b, 1989) provides an excellent introduction to the broad nature of student outcomes research, the design of longitudinal data bases, and the use and limitations of indicators. Those seeking more specific information on the construction of computerized student cohort files should consult the LONESTAR implementation manual (Ewell, Parker, and Jones, 1988) as well as LONESTAR's data element dictionary (National Center for Higher Education Management Systems, 1988). Finally, Bers (1989) provides a collection of essays focusing on the problems community colleges confront in developing student tracking systems. She and her associates note the need for tracking systems, cite examples of college efforts in this area, and detail the obstacles that need to be overcome.

******

Alkin, M. C. Development of an Integrated Information System. Sacramento: Office of the Chancellor, California Community Colleges, 1985. (ED 273 326)

Astin, A. W. Four Critical Years: Effects of College on Beliefs, Attitudes and Knowledge. San Francisco: Jossey-Bass, 1977.

Astin, A. W. Minorities in American Higher Education: Recent Trends, Current Prospects, and Recommendations. San Francisco: Jossey-Bass, 1982.

Baldwin, A. Dual Enrollment High School Students: A Longitudinal Study of the 1982-83 Cohort. Research Report No. 88-04. Miami, Fla.: Miami-Dade Community College, 1988. (ED 293 579)

Baker, C. O., and Ogle, L. T. (Eds.) The Condition of Education, 1989, Volume II, Postsecondary Education. CS 89-650. Washington, D.C.: U.S. Department of Education, Office of Educational Research and Improvement, 1989.

Banta, T. W. "Editor's Notes." In T. W. Banta (Ed.), Implementing Outcomes Assessment: Promise and Perils. New Directions for Institutional Research, No. 59. San Francisco: Jossey-Bass, 1988.

Belcher, M. Institutional Effectiveness at Miami-Dade Community College. Research Report No. 89-11R. Miami, Fla.: Miami-Dade Community College, 1989.

Belcher, M. J. Success of Students Who Begin College by Enrolling in English as a Second Language. Research Report No. 88-09. Miami, Fla.: Miami-Dade Community College, 1988. (ED 296 763).

Bers, T. H., and Rubin, A. M. "Tracking Students in Community Colleges: The Unreported Challenges." In T. H. Bers (Ed.), Using Student Tracking Systems Effectively. New Directions for Community Colleges, No. 66. San Francisco: Jossey-Bass, 1989.

Bers, T. H. (Ed.). Using Student Tracking Systems Effectively. New Directions for Community Colleges, No. 66. San Francisco: Jossey-Bass, 1989.

Borow, H., and Hendrix, V. L. Environmental Differentials of Occupational Programs and Educational Career Patterns in Public Junior Colleges. Minneapolis: Department of Educational Administration, University of Minnesota, 1974. (ED 105 910).

Bragg, A.K. "Beyond the College: State Policy Impact on Student Tracking Systems." In T. Bers (Ed.), Using Student Tracking Systems Effectively. New Directions for Community Colleges, No. 66. San Francisco: Jossey-Bass, 1989.

Brawer, F. B. "Assessing Student Goals and Outcomes." Paper presented at the Maryland Deans' Meeting, Arnold, Md., March 25, 1988. (ED 292 486).

California Commission for the Review of the Master Plan for Higher Education. The Challenge of Change: A Reassessment of the California Community Colleges. Sacramento: The Commission, 1986. (ED 269 048).

California Community Colleges. Student Matriculation: A Plan for Implementation in the California Community Colleges. Sacramento: California Community Colleges, Board of Governors, 1984. (ED 261 738).

California Postsecondary Education Commission. Feasibility Plan for a Comprehensive Student Information Study. A Report to the Legislature and Governor in Response to Assembly Bill 880 (1984). Commission Report 86-8. Sacramento; California Postsecondary Education Commission, 1986.

Carroll, C. D. College Persistence and Degree Attainment for 1980 High School Graduates: Hazards for Transfer, Dropout, and Part-Timers. CS 89-302. Washington, D.C.: National Center for Education Statistics, 1989.

Carter, E. H. "Meeting the Challenge of Change: An Opportunity for Research in the Community College." In J. Losak (Ed.), Applying Institutional Research in Decision Making. New Directions for Community Colleges, No. 56. San Francisco: Jossey-Bass, 1986.

Clagett, C.A. Student Outcomes Performance Accountability Report. Largo, Md.: Prince George's Community College, 1988.

Coffey, J.C. "From Access to Accountability: Community Colleges and Student Tracking." Working paper prepared for the AACJC FIPSE Project on Student Tracking, January 5, 1989.

Coffey, J.C. Proving What We're Doing Is Working: The Student Flow Research Model. Sacramento: Los Rios Community College District, 1987. (ED 279 379).

Cohen, A. M., and Brawer, F. B. The American Community College. San Francisco: Jossey-Bass, 1982.

Cohen, A. M., and Brawer, F. B. The American Community College. Second Edition. San Francisco: Jossey-Bass, 1989.

Cohen, A. M., and Brawer, F. B. The Collegiate Function of Community Colleges. San Francisco: Jossey-Bass, 1987.

Community College of Philadelphia. Entering Student Goals, 1985-86 Academic Year [and] Enrollment Goals and Progress Toward Goal Accomplishment: A Snapshot of the 1985-86 Student Body. Philadelphia, Pa.: Community College of Philadelphia, 1987. (ED 293 570).

Community College of Philadelphia. Student Flow of the 1982 Graduates. Office of Institutional Research Report # 23. Philadelphia, Pa.: Community College of Philadelphia, 1982. (ED 256 384).

Doucette, D. S. and Teeter, D.J. "Student Mobility Among the Public Community Colleges and Universities in the State of Kansas." Paper presented at the Annual Forum of the Association for Institutional Research, Portland, Ore., April 28-May 1, 1985. (ED 262 844).

Eagle, E., Fitzgerald, R. A., Gifford, A., and Tuma, J. National Longitudinal Study 1972. A Descriptive Summary of 1972 High School Seniors: Fourteen Years Later. Contractor Report. CS 88-406. Washington, D.C.: National Center for Education Statistics, 1988.

Edwards, F. L. and Staatse, H. Fall 1980 Cohort Study. Technical Report 85-06. Trenton, N.J.: Mercer County Community College, 1985. (ED 261 749).

Ewell, P. T. "About Halfway: Assessment at the Balance Point." Assessment Update, 1989, 1 (1), 1-2, 4-7.

Ewell, P. T. "Establishing a Computer-Based Assessment Program." In D. F. Halpern (Ed.). Student Outcomes Assessment: What Institutions Stand to Gain. New Directions for Higher Education, No. 59. San Francisco: Jossey-Bass, 1987a.

Ewell, P. T. Information on Student Outcomes: How to Get It and How to Use It. Boulder, Colo.: National Center for Higher Education Management Systems, 1983. 89 pp. (ED 246 827).

Ewell, P. T. "Principles of Longitudinal Enrollment Analysis: Conducting Retention and Student Flow Studies." In Muffo, S. A., and McLaughlin, G. W. (Eds.), A Primer on Institutional Research. Tallahassee, Fla.: Association for Institutional Research, 1987b.

Ewell, P. T., Parker, R., and Jones, D. Establishing A Longitudinal Student Tracking System: An Implementation Handbook. Boulder, Colo.: National Center for Higher Education Management Systems, 1988.

Farland, R. W., Anderson, B., and Boakes, B. Vocational Education Student Follow-Up System for

Information. Sacramento: Office of the Chancellor, California Community Colleges, 1987. (ED 280 525).

Florida Community College at Jacksonville. Strategic Performance Indicators. Jacksonville, Fla.: Florida Community College at Jacksonville, 1989.

Hamre, W., and Holsclaw, M. 1989-90 Implementation of the Management Information System. [Sacramento]: Board of Governors of the California Community Colleges, 1989.

Hawk, T. R. "Quality Assessment in Action." Paper presented at the Annual Meeting of the Pennsylvania Community Colleges, June 1987. (ED 293 575).

Illinois Community College Board. Current Issues in Transfer Articulation Between Community Colleges and Four-Year Colleges and Universities in Illinois. Springfield: Illinois Community College Board, 1989.

Illinois Community College Board. Illinois Community College Board Transfer Study: A Five-Year Study of Students Transferring from Illinois Two-Year Colleges to Illinois Senior Colleges/ Universities in the Fall of 1979. Springfield: Illinois Community College Board, 1986. (ED 270 148).

Illinois Community College Board. Illinois Community Colleges Statewide Occupational Student Follow-Up Study: Final Report of a Three-Year Longitudinal Study of Fall 1974 New Students Enrolled in Occupational Programs. Springfield: Illinois Community College Board, 1979. (ED 169 958).

Johnson County Community College. Kansas Community Colleges Class of 1987: Five-Year Longitudinal Study. Two-Year Interim Report. Overland Park, Kans.: Johnson County Community College, 1987. (ED 880 040).

Kitchens, H. M. Statewide Longitudinal Study: Initial Report. Cheyenne: Wyoming Community College Commission, 1987. (ED 291 433).

Koefoed, J. O., Jr. "An Examination of the Goals of Incoming Students at Kirkwood Community College." Ed. D. Major Applied Research Project, Nova University, 1985. (ED 262 848).

Lach, I. J., Kohl, P., and Wellman, F. Follow-Up Study of FY 1978 Occupational Graduates of the Illinois Public Community Colleges. Springfield: Illinois Community College Board, 1979. (ED 176 823).

League for Innovation in the Community College. "Assessing Institutional Effectiveness in the Community College." Unpublished first draft, Laguna Hills, Calif.: League for Innovation in the Community College, 1989.

Lee, B. S. Measures of Progress, 1984-1987: A Four-Year Retrospective. Sacramento, Calif.: Los Rios Community College District, Office of Research and Planning, 1987.

Lucas, J. A. Longitudinal Study of Performance of Students Entering Harper College, 1974-1984. Research Report Series Volume XIV, No. 6. Palatine, Ill.: William Rainey Harper College, 1986. (ED 264 931).

McCabe, R. H. A Status Report of the Comprehensive Educational Reform of Miami-Dade Community College. Miami, Fla.: Miami-Dade Community College, 1983. (ED 259 770).

McCabe, R. H. "Now is the Time to Reform the American Community College." Community and Junior College Journal, 1981, 51 (8), 6-10.

Maryland State Board for Community Colleges. Performance Profile, Maryland Community Colleges. Annapolis: Maryland State Board for Community Colleges, 1988. (ED 297 807).

Meznek, J., and Murdoch, A. Matriculation: Preliminary Report on First-Year Implementation. Sacramento: California Community Colleges, Office of the Chancellor, 1989. (ED 302 307).

Miami-Dade Community College. Miami-Dade Community College 1984 Institutional Self-Study. Volume II: Prescriptive Education. Miami, Fla.: Miami-Dade Community College, 1985. (ED 259 770).

Montemayor, J. J., and others. Glendale Community College Students' Educational Intent Survey, Spring 1985. Research Report 1. Glendale, Ariz.: Glendale Community College, 1985. (ED 281 572).

Moore, K. M. "Assessment of Institutional Effectiveness." In J. Losak (Ed.), Applying Institutional Research in Decision Making. New Directions for Community Colleges, No. 56. San Francisco: Jossey-Bass, 1986.

Morris, C., and Losak, J. Student Success at Miami-Dade Community College: Issues and Data. Research Report No. 86-22. Miami, Fla.: Miami-Dade Community College, 1986.

Moss, J. S.I.Q. — Student Information Questionnaire: A Survey of Student Characteristics, Fall 1984. San Francisco: San Francisco Community College District, 1985. (ED 257 487).

National Center for Education Statistics. Baccalaureate and Beyond Study. Position Paper, November 1988. [Washington, D.C.]: U. S. Department of Education, 1988.

National Center for Higher Education Management Systems. LONESTAR: Texas Community Colleges Student Tracking System. Pilot Test Version 1.2. Data Element Dictionary. Boulder, Colo.: National Center for Higher Education Management Systems, 1988a. (ED 302 273).

National Center for Higher Education Management Systems. LONESTAR: Texas Community Colleges Student Tracking System. Pilot Test Version 1.2. Implementation Manual. Boulder, Colo.: National Center for Higher Education Management Systems, 1988b. (ED 302 272)

Palmer, J. "Assessing the Employment Experiences of Community College Vocational Program

Graduates: A Review of Institutional Follow-Up Studies." Graduate Seminar Paper, UCLA, 1985 (ED 258 665).

Palmer, J. "Setting the AACJC Research Agenda." Community, Technical, and Junior College Journal, 1988, 58 (4), pp. 32-34, 43.

Renkiewicz, N., Hamre, B., and Lewis, M. Indicators and Measures of Successful Community Colleges. A Report to the 59th Annual CACC Convention, November 1988. Sacramento: California Association of Community Colleges, 1988. (ED 301 286).

Roesler, E. D. Assessment of Institutional Effectiveness: A Position Paper Prepared for the Committee on the Future of the Virginia Community College System. Richmond: Virginia State Department of Community Colleges, 1988. (ED 297 806).

Romano, R. (Comp.). A Statistical Profile of the Entering Class at Broome Community College, Fall 1983: Student Characteristics, Needs, and Goals. Working Paper Series No. 1-85. Binghamton, N.Y.: Institute for Community College Research, Broome Community College, 1985. (ED 263 972).

Sheldon, M. Stephen. Statewide Longitudinal Study: Report on Academic Year[s] 1978-81. Part 5: Final Report. Woodland Hills, Calif.: Los Angeles Pierce College, 1982. (ED 217 917).

Sheldon, M. S., and Grafton, C. L. "Raison d'Etre: Students." Community and Junior College Journal, 1982, 53 (3), 19-20.

Simmons, H. L. "Institutional Effectiveness in the Community College: Assessing Institutional Effectiveness through the Accreditation Process." Paper presented at the League for Innovation in the Community College Conference, Charlotte, N.C., July 17-20, 1988. (ED 297 825).

Voorhees, R. A., and Hart, S. "A Tracking Scheme for Basic Skills Intake Assessment." In T. H. Bers (Ed.), Using Student Tracking Systems Effectively. New Directions for Community Colleges, No. 66. San Francisco: Jossey-Bass, 1989.

Wilkinson, R. "Outcomes and Impacts: A Student Tracking Study for Eastern New Mexico University." Paper collected as part of the American Association for Higher Education Assessment Forum, 1985. (ED 285 451).

Wilms, W. W., and Hansell, S. "The Dubious Promise of Postsecondary Vocational Education: Its Payoff to Dropouts and Graduates in the U.S.A." International Journal of Educational Development, 1982, 2, 42-59.

Wyoming Community College Commission. Statewide Longitudinal Study Interim Report. Cheyenne: Wyoming Community College Commission, 1988. (ED 297 833).